EVERGREEN PACIFIC
PUBLISHING

SHELLFISH GUIDE

FROM CATCHING TO COOKING, YOUR COMPLETE WEST COAST GUIDE FOR:

- CRAB • OYSTERS • CALAMARI • SQUID
- CLAMS • CRAWFISH • MUSSELS

SECOND EDITION
by J.D. Wade

Credits

All photos and illustrations with the parenthetical (WDFW) were provided by the Washington State Department of Fish & Wildlife.

Cover photo, design and layout: Herb Collingridge IV.

Photos on page 54 by Barry Gregg.

All other photos were provided by the author.

Maps on pages 47-49 were provided by the author and Lee Wade.

All other illustrations were provided by Lee Wade.

Published by Evergreen Pacific Publishing, 4204 Russell Road, Suite M, Mukilteo, WA 98275.

ISBN 978-1-934707-05-0

Text was typeset in FF Scala regular. Cover title set in AT Sackers Gothic heavy.

WARNINGS

If the water in the area from which you are harvesting shellfish is contaminated, most likely the shellfish will also be contaminated, and sometimes an area normally free of contamination can suddenly become polluted. For example, a major rainstorm can overflow storm drains or sewage treatment plants, causing pollutants to flow into normally pristine waters. Refer to the chapter on "toxins," and note the important phone numbers to call before harvesting shellfish.

Several beaches and shellfish harvesting areas are identified on the charts in this book. Please note that public accessibility to a beach can change at any time. For example, litigation may result in a "public" beach becoming a private beach, or a beach or area may be declared closed to shellfishing by a government agency. Watch for posted signs in any area in which you intend to harvest shellfish. At times a beach may be open to the public, but the property above the beach will be private. Please respect the rights of the property owners. To check the status of a beach or area for harvesting shellfish, refer to the numbers listed in the appendixes of this book.

The charts in this book are offered only as reference to where different shellfhis species are normally found. They should not be considered showing where they can be accessed, due to private properties, closed beaches, or water quality problems.

CONTENTS

ABOUT THE AUTHOR

J.D. Wade is a lifetime resident of the Puget Sound area in Washington state. He began playing and digging on shellfish beaches at an early age. As an adult he helped organize a Hood Canal seafood business, harvesting clams and oysters for private beach owners. He also was a commercial prawn fisherman and owned a retail/wholesale seafood store, supplying fresh shellfish to the local public plus markets and restaurants.

J.D. has become a strong, vocal advocate of shellfish conservation and is well known by Washington state legislators, having testified many times on seafood conservation issues before the House and Senate Natural Resources Committees.

As a popular outdoor writer for over 25 years, with weekly newspaper and monthly magazine columns, he keeps his finger on the pulse of Northwest shellfish issues.

J.D. has been a sought-after speaker at the Seattle Boat Show as well as many other sportsman's shows around the state. In this role, J.D. promotes the fun of shellfishing while at the same time supporting the conservation of our fragile resources.

INTRODUCTION

The northwest coast of North America is known for rugged natural beauty and abundant sea life. Its mild climate and clean ocean waters produce a home for a rich variety of marine life, including hundreds of species of shellfish.

Boaters and beachcombers thrive upon the tasty inhabitants of these waters and shores, taking great pride and enjoyment in gathering their own food from the environment.

Gathering shellfish is an outstanding family activity. Experiencing nature outdoors together is both bonding and rewarding, and the outcome will be a delicious meal. Even people who do not care for the flavor of fish, usually enjoy a good fresh shellfish dinner.

The anticipation of pulling up a crab trap is exciting. Digging in the sand in pursuit of a clam is therapeutic. Counting the number of shrimp in the trap that just came aboard can be rewarding or disappointing, but never boring. Kids love the activities.

This book is intended to present to the recreational shellfish gatherer an overview of the most popular types of edible shellfish, what type of areas to locate them in, and how to harvest, cook and eat them. Included in this book are suggested recipes for preparing your catch while still on the beach, back at your campsite, aboard your boat, or at home.

The Shellfish Guide will explore not only gathering, but storing, cooking and eating your culinary rewards. The reader will learn the best ways to do it all. Hopefully shellfish gathering will become a family adventure that will lead to many years of togetherness and healthy meals.

Plan the outing by studying charts together and making a list of necessary tools and baits required. Don't forget safety and comfort items. Life vests, warm clothes and snacks are as important as the tools needed for a fun family outing. A wet, cold, and hungry experience might leave a lasting negative impression, but proper preparation will yield an enjoyable experience which everyone will want to repeat.

Enjoy, and *bon appetit.*

CLAMS

There are many species of clams along North America's west coast, but only a handful are of interest to recreational boaters and sportsmen. They are found on the open coast and in inland bays and harbors. Although clams can be found in nearly all areas, it's getting increasingly difficult to distinguish public beaches from private. Much care must be exercised in determining where it is legal and proper to dig for these delicious nuggets. Usually government-owned tidelands are open for harvest. (See charts included in this chapter and the appendixes.)

Clams are subterranean water filters. They are called "intertidal" shellfish, in that they live in that area between the lowest tide and the highest tide. They live under the beaches, drawing water through their siphon-like necks and filtering out food particles, primarily plankton. The water is then discharged back toward the surface. In sandy or muddy beaches this discharge creates water geysers at low tides, or holes, which give away the clam's location.

This filtering action creates another concern. Clams filter out and retain pollutants from the water, so one must consider the environmental conditions before harvesting and eating clams.

In this chapter we will look at clam species in order of desirability: Razor Clams, Littleneck Clams, known as "steamers," Butter Clams, Geoduck, and Horse Clams.

RAZOR CLAMS:

This variety of beach dwellers has a sweet, succulent flavor, causing it to be widely considered the world's best tasting clam. Razor clams can be found on sandy beaches of coastline from northern California to

Siliqua Patual, alias Razor Clam, have thin elongated shells covered with a shiny, tan periostracum (skin).

Common Inter-tidal Clams

Butter clam
Saxidomus giganteus
Average size is 3-4", up to 6". Shells are usually chalky-white with no radiating ridges. The siphon can be pulled into its shell. Usually found 12-18" below the surface.

Native littleneck clam
Protothaca staminea
Average size is 1-2", up to 2-1/2". Rounded shell has concentric and radiating lines. Found 6-10" below surface.

(Not to scale)

Cockle clam
Clinocardium nuttali
Prominent, evenly-spaced ridges which fan out from the hinge. Mottled, light brown. Can grow to 5". Found just below surface.

Horse clam
Tresus capax (shown)
Tresus nuttalli (not shown)
Large, can be up to 8". Shell is chalky-white with yellow-brown patches of "skin." The siphon can't be pulled into shell and has a leather-like flap on the tip. Found 1-2 feet below surface.

(WDFW—illustrations provided to WDFW by Roby Bowman, Debbie Bacon, and Darrell Pruett)

(Eastern) Softshell clam
Mya arenaria
Can grow to 6". Shells are soft, chalky-white with a rough, irregular surface. Shell is rounded at the foot end, pointed at the siphon end. Found to 18" below surface.

Manila littleneck clam
Tapes philippinarum
Average size is 1-2", up to 2-1/2". Oblong shell has concentric and radiating lines. May have colored patterned shells. Found to 4" below surface.

Geoduck clam
Panopea abrupta
Heavy, oblong shell, rounded at one end. Appears cut-off at the other. The siphon can't be retracted. Found 2-3 feet below surface. Can weigh up to 10 lbs.

Alaska's Aleutian Islands. They are always found below Mean Low Low Water, which means you can only harvest them during "'minus" low tides. They will usually be found near the sand's surface, but that does not mean they are easy to catch. Yes, I said "catch." They can move FAST!

Siliqua Patula, as they are known in science books, reach maturity in just two years, growing to an average of four and a half inches in length and two inches in width. These tasty delicacies are prized by the public, and are hardly ever found in seafood stores. Consequently thousands of people gather on beaches during open season low tides. In order to protect the clam population, seasons are very restricted. In Washington state there is no commercial harvest allowed except by tribes. In Oregon and B.C. very limited commercial harvest is allowed by non-tribal individuals.

Refer to the local game regulations for seasons and bag limits. Whatever the limit, diggers must keep the first number of clams to meet

The Washington State Limit for Razor Clams is 15 clams. Note the shellfish license which is required to be worn visibly when digging clams or crab fishing. (WDFW)

People crowd the beaches for a single day at a time of Razor Clam harvest. (WDFW)

the state limits. Small clams can't be discarded in order to fill a limit with bigger clams.

Since razor clams taste so good and the season is so restricted, let's look at how you can make the best use of your time to catch your limit. Suppose a season opening has been announced and you've driven your family to the beach, equipped with all the proper shellfish licenses and equipment. Each person needs his or her own container for holding a separate clam limit. The digging implement can be shared, but remember, you will only have a short time to dig. No more than two persons should share one tool between them.

The best digging time will be an hour before to an hour after the low tide. If the tide is before daylight, good lights are a must. Headlamps combined with lanterns are handy. Flashlights are clumsy because you need both hands free for digging. Since you are at the water's edge, anything you lay on the sand is vulnerable to incoming waves. Yes, sometimes you can get wet when on your knees and about to catch up with a fleeing clam, and the unnoticed wave approaches. It's all part of the fun. A change of shoes, socks and pants is handy to have on hand.

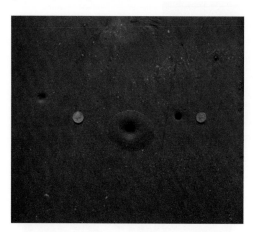

Clam vent holes are called a "show." Usually the larger show means a larger clam. The center show with a "halo" means the clam is close to the surface. Note the dimes for size comparison. (WDFW)

You will be looking for the "show." No, it's not movie time. The show here is a depression in the sand, or a hole. The larger the show the larger the clam that made it. These shows are made when the tip of the clams neck, which is close to the surface, is retracted, causing the depression, or when it "vents" itself when feeding, creating the hole. You can make the clam show itself by stomping around in ten-foot diameter circles, then watching for a show. Kids love doing this, but they may not be heavy enough to make the show. However, it does burn off energy, which is always good to do at the beach.

How to Dig With a Clam Shovel

1. Place the shovel blade 4 to 6 inches seaward of the clam show. The handle of the shovel should be pointed toward the sand dunes.

(WDFW)

2. Use your body weight to push the shovel blade straight into the sand while you drop to one knee. In hard sand, gently rock the shovel handle from side to side for ease of entry. It is very important to keep the blade as vertical as possible to keep from breaking the clam shell.

(WDFW)

3. Pull the handle back just enough to break the suction in the sand, still keeping the blade as straight as possible. The sand will crack as shown.

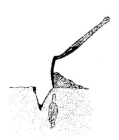

(WDFW)

4. Succeeding scoops of sand expose the clam enough to reach down with your hand and grasp its shell. Razor clams move rapidly downward but not; horizontally. Make sure you keep the first 15 clams and avoid wasting any.

(WDFW)

A "clam gun" is a very specialized shovel tool, designed just for digging razor clams. Its long narrow blade is angled just right for chasing fast-moving clams, and it has a short, stout handle. Most good clam diggers will open a hole in the sand on the water side of the show, then drop to their knees, and dig like a dog burying a bone, as fast as possible. This way the elusive clam can be felt and retrieved without breaking its shell.

Newer modern technology brought about the invention of the "clam tube." This is a hollow, metal, two-foot-long tube, four inches in diameter. It's open on one end, closed on the other, with a half inch air vent hole and handles.

(WDFW)

Facing the ocean, you should center the clam tube over the show, slant the top of the tube slightly toward yourself and push down with a rocking or twisting motion. (Leave the air vent uncovered.) This will keep you in line with the clam's descent. Work the tube down 6 to 10 inches. Then cover the air vent and pull up. Use your leg muscles, keeping the back straight to avoid muscle strain. Release the air vent, emptying the tube, then go back down the hole another six or eight inches after the clam. The suction created by pulling the sand out of the hole can be quite heavy. Take your time with this method. The clam will not out-dig you. You may remove two or more sand cores from the tube before catching the clam. Check each core that you bring up: the clam may be concealed within. Even though this method was designed to make razor clam digging easier, there are definite drawbacks. The tube is only four inches wide, allowing less then an inch of clearance on either side of mature clams, leading to many broken shells. Back muscle strain is common and even heart attacks can be brought on from the effort of lifting. Be cautious and take your time. Rest a lot between "battles." Since their shells can be easily broken by contact with digging implements or rough handling

Kids love digging clams. (WDFW)

during the battle, most agencies require you to keep every razor clam dug, regardless of size or condition, and the states requests that you fill all your holes.

Tip: For the safety of humans and beach dwellers, always fill in your holes when digging for any species of clam. The fresh pile of material removed from your excavation may plug the airway of whatever creature is living beneath the beach surface, leading to death. Some clam-digging tides occur at night, and open holes in the darkness are obvious human safety hazards. If the incoming tide covers a hole, someone can take a nasty, wet tumble.

Your limit caught, it's time to clean your clams. All razor clams should be cleaned before cooking. Remove the meat by simply submerging clams in boiling water for a few seconds, or pouring boiling water over them. When the shell pops open, put them immediately into cold water and remove the meat. Another way is to cut the four attachments of the paired adductor muscles by running a knife blade along the inner surface of each shell. The basic aim in cleaning is to remove the gills and digestive tract, the dark parts of the clam. The following commercial procedure for "steaking" clams for frying is done with a sharp knife or scissors.

"Pea Crab" are found under the shells of some species of large clams. They pose no health threat to either the host clam or humans. Simply discard them.

Snip off the tip of the neck.

Cut open the body from the base of the neck.

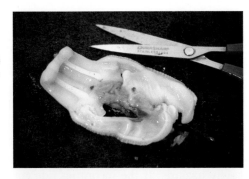

The gills and foot are separated with two cuts.

A circular cut of the foot will remove the gut. After removing the gut, slit the foot so it lies flat.

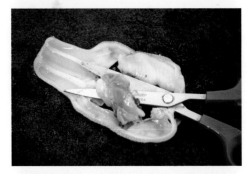

Rinse, and the steak is ready for further preparation.

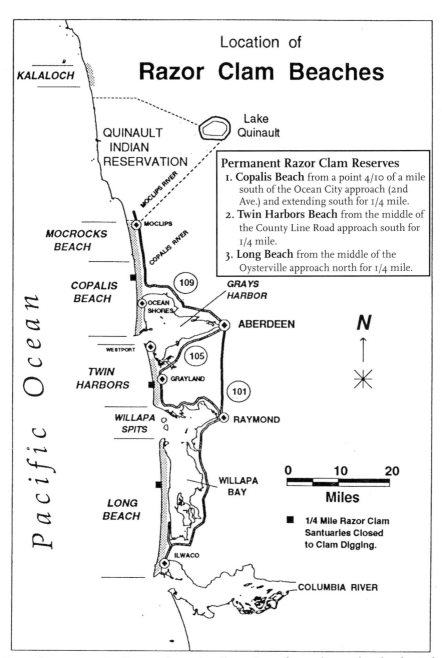

Location of Razor Clam Beaches

KALALOCH

QUINAULT INDIAN RESERVATION

Lake Quinault

Permanent Razor Clam Reserves
1. **Copalis Beach** from a point 4/10 of a mile south of the Ocean City approach (2nd Ave.) and extending south for 1/4 mile.
2. **Twin Harbors Beach** from the middle of the County Line Road approach south for 1/4 mile.
3. **Long Beach** from the middle of the Oysterville approach north for 1/4 mile.

MOCROCKS BEACH

MOCLIPS RIVER

MOCLIPS

COPALIS RIVER

COPALIS BEACH

OCEAN SHORES

109

GRAYS HARBOR

ABERDEEN

WESTPORT

105

TWIN HARBORS

GRAYLAND

101

WILLAPA SPITS

RAYMOND

Pacific Ocean

WILLAPA BAY

LONG BEACH

ILWACO

COLUMBIA RIVER

N

0   10   20
Miles

■ 1/4 Mile Razor Clam Santuaries Closed to Clam Digging.

Razor clam sanctuaries (Reserves) are 1/4 mile sections of coastal ocean beaches located on three beach areas that are used to assist in the management of the razor clam resource. The three areas are marked with large metal or wooden posts and are adequately signed to designate a no-digging area. Sampling occurs on a continuing basis for various population studies and comparisons with harvested areas.

LITTLENECK CLAMS ("STEAMERS"):

There are two types of little neck clams on the west coast: the native one, and a hybrid import from Japan known as "Manila." All these succulent little nuggets are easy to find, easy to harvest, and wonderful table fare.

Littleneck clams can be found on the coastline from lower California to Alaska. They are main dinner courses for thousands of boaters and beach combing campers each year. Native littlenecks are small, seldom more then two inches wide, and vary in color from white to grey to light brown. They are indigenous to the Northwest and can be found on gravel beaches, usually ones which contain some small to pea-size stones, to which the larvae can safely attach during spawn cycles. They are very prolific. When the spawns occur, the larvae can spread up to fifty miles, drifting along with the currents. This is how the imported Japanese Manila variety has spread throughout the Northwest. Lying alongside the natives in many of the same beds, the Manilas are a different color. Dark purple to black, with white or yellowish marbling, they are also more oblong in shape. Normally they will be found between mid-tide to low-tide ranges. These clams will seldom be found more than six inches below the beach surface, and, unlike other clam species, will rarely be found on sandy beaches.

(WDFW)

Top Left: Eastern Soft-shell Clam (pointed)
Top Right: Butter Clam
Center: Cockle
Lower Left: Manilla Clam
Lower Right: Native Littleneck Clam

TIP: Littlenecks can be found under beach boulders. Roll the stone aside and check the bottom of the remaining depression.

TIP: Most of the time, you will find littleneck clams under any oyster beds you encounter.

TIP: Clams must be kept alive until time to cook. Keep them cool and damp. If possible, keep them in a bag suspended in salt water. This will also "purge" them, allowing them to naturally flush out sand. A better way to purge them is to place them in a bucket of salt water and throw in a handful of corn meal. They will take in the meal, expelling their grit. The shell normally will be closed, as long as they are alive, or will quickly close when touched. Discard any that do not close before cooking. After cooking the shell should be open. Discard any still closed after cooking because that is also an indication that the clam was dead before cooking.

BUTTER CLAMS:

These are the big and husky specimens of the sweet clam family. They have thick shells growing to five-inch diameters, and hang out deeper underground. They have an excellent flavor, making them worth the extra digging effort required to harvest them. *They are also particularly good at storing toxins and pollutants, holding them many months longer than other species.* Be aware of local conditions when harvesting them.

Butter clams can be found near the low water mark on a variety of beach surfaces. You will find them in sand, pea gravel, or even between large rocks on a gravel beach. If the tide is not low enough, you will need to look in the water, as they can be found in water up to depths of 60 feet.

Small butter clams are often mistaken for littlenecks because they can be found near the surface along with littlenecks, and taste nearly as good. Their color will vary, depending upon the surrounding sand or gravel colors. Primarily greyish-white, they can be yellow, brown, or even black.

Just as other clam populations seem to be in colonies, butters will be found in clumps. Where there is one, more will be nearby, with the larger ones lying deeper, under the smaller.

COCKLE CLAMS:

The cockle clam is so similar to littleneck clams and the butter clam that it is hard to distinguish among them, especially when wet and covered with sand or mud. Only with two different kinds of these clams side by side can you tell the cockle clam by its more pronounced ridges. It can be found in the same habitat and cooked in the same manner as steamers and butter clams.

TIP: Littleneck clams, butter clams, and cockle clams, unlike razor clams, have a size limit. (Consult your state shellfish regulations.) If the clam is under the limit size, place the clam back in the hole in which you found it.

HORSE CLAMS:

The common view of these abundant, thin-shelled, deep-digging bivalves is that they are large, tasteless. and tough. Most folks think the only good use for a horse clam is as crab or bottomfish bait. Actually, they are quite flavorful when used in chowder.

Adult horse clams can reach 8 inches in diameter, and are found one to two feet deep on sandy beaches, in the lowest third of tidal zones. Because their siphons (necks) are so long, they can squirt fountains of water into the air at low tide, and still be so deep it will take an excavation to dig them out. They range from California to Alaska.

Their shells are white, with a thin brownish covering that easily flakes off when exposed to the air. Because their necks are so long, horse clams frequently are mistaken for geoducks. They can

Horse Clams   (WDFW)

be distinguished by the tip of the neck being leathery and usually covered with barnacles, whereas the geoduck has smooth skin over its entire neck.

TIP: Pea crabs are typically found under the shells of large species of clams. They are tiny little white crawlies, with soft shells of less then an inch in diameter, and completely harmless to humans or their host clams. Simply discard them.

GEODUCK CLAMS:

Pronounced "goo-ee-duck," these huge, ugly clam monsters are tastier than they appear. They are only found during the very lowest tides of the year, in sandy or muddy beaches, dug in at 18-inch to four foot depths. Their average weight is a meal-size 2-1/2 pounds, with larger specimens being common. They are such a popular clam that areas regularly accessible to diggers are wiped out, and only during the lowest minus tides (minus 2 feet or better) are the untouched beds accessible. Extreme minus tides like these occur perhaps 20 times a year, further restricting the sport harvest.

Geoducks can be found by spotting their siphon sticking out of the ground, but they are most easily seen while still underwater. They can be harvested quite efficiently by divers, or you may locate some while snorkeling. When you discover one, another will be nearby. Bed densities can be as high as one per square foot. They prefer areas with a soft sand and mud bottom, which further limits accessibility. They cannot tolerate the higher salinity of the ocean, and therefore are found only in bays and canals, but not along the coast. A five-year-old geoduck shell measures five and a half inches, but the siphon (neck) often extends up to 36 inches.

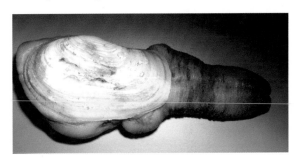

Geoduck Clam

(WDFW)

DIGGING GEODUCKS: Do you know where you can borrow a steam shovel? The huge reward you will gain when you finally get one of these giant clams out of the ground will be worth the effort, but it will be effort. Hard work and muddy clothes will be part of the price you pay.

Kids have a ball doing this type of thing. Don your best Tom Sawyer face and provide them with a shovel with a long sturdy handle. You can tell them the popular story that the geoduck is trying to flee and is digging down as fast as it can. Actually, it doesn't move much, but as it retracts its siphon-like neck, it gives the impression of trying to out-dig the sand-flinging shoveler with clam chowder on his mind.

Most folks dig a trench alongside the clam, deep enough to get below the shell, then cave the trench in, searching for the dinner entree. Don't pull on the neck; you'll pull it off, and it's illegal to possess only a geoduck neck. Just keep probing and digging until you free the whole object. Rinse it off and store it in a wet gunny sack. Daily limit in most areas is three.

CLEANING: The neck can be cut up or ground up in chowder, after rinsing out sand and grit. The body meat, sliced open and entrails removed, can be pounded flat and sauteed, resembling abalone.

COMMERCIAL GRADING: Markets always drive the commercial demand in seafood products. A 50-pound halibut is worth three times as much wholesale as a 100-plus-pound fish. But in that example, the reason the smaller fish is more valuable is that the meat has better flavor and texture. Unfortunately, with geoduck, all grades have the same flavor and texture, the only difference is in the skin color.

A geoduck with a creamy-white skin color is considered Number 1 grade. A tan color is Number 2, and black is a nearly worthless Number 3. Commercial harvesters work in diving suits connected by air hoses to a tender boat, and use high pressure water hoses to blow the sand and mud away from the quarry. The work is performed by feel in murky, sometimes deep, water. The color grades cannot be determined until the bags of clams are dumped on the tender deck. The lower grades cannot be returned to the bottom: they would just die. By law, they must be retained with the catch. Why the different grades? All I can explain is the majority of the catch is sold in Asian markets and there, to women shoppers. They just will not purchase a dark-necked clam, even though it is exactly as tasty as a lighter skinned product. So, if you can find a dark specimen for sale at reduced price, don't hesitate to grab the bargain.

(EASTERN) SOFTSHELL CLAMS:

The softshell clam got its name because of its chalky white, fragile shell. The shell is rounded at the foot end and tapered at the siphon end. Because of its chalky-white shell and because its siphon cannot be completely withdrawn, softshell clams are often mistaken for small horse clams. Softshell clams average four to six inches in length and are found on muddy or sandy beaches, often near the mouths of rivers. They are buried to a depth of eight to eighteen inches. Like the horse clam, they are known more for their use as crab or bottomfish bait than as an edible delicacy.

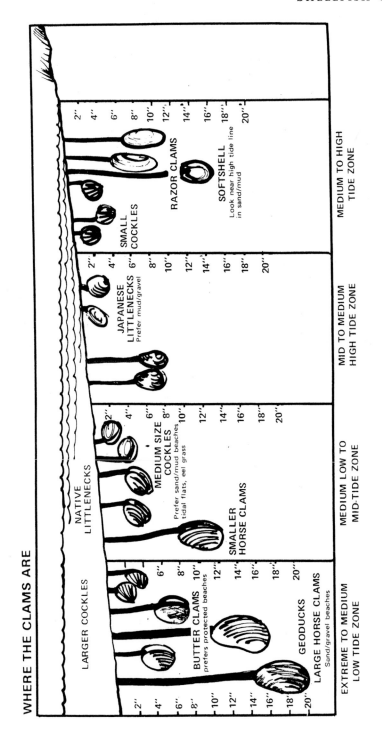

WHERE THE CLAMS ARE

LARGER COCKLES

NATIVE LITTLENECKS

SMALL COCKLES

JAPANESE LITTLENECKS
Prefer mud/gravel

RAZOR CLAMS

SOFTSHELL
Look near high tide line in sand/mud

MEDIUM SIZE COCKLES
Prefer sand/mud beaches tidal flats, eel grass

SMALLER HORSE CLAMS

BUTTER CLAMS
prefers protected beaches

GEODUCKS

LARGE HORSE CLAMS
Sand/gravel beaches

MEDIUM TO HIGH TIDE ZONE

MID TO MEDIUM HIGH TIDE ZONE

MEDIUM LOW TO MID-TIDE ZONE

EXTREME TO MEDIUM LOW TIDE ZONE

CRABS

How can something as mean looking as a crab taste so good? One of the most popular family outdoor activities is crab fishing. Kids of all ages love doing it, and the end result is usually a crab-eating festivity.

The North American west coast has abundant numbers of Dungeness and Red Rock Crab creating a multimillion dollar commercial harvest industry and a huge sportfishing industry. Crab are very important to the economy and they are really fun to catch. Let's take a look at how and where to find these tasty crustaceans.

Any body of salt water which has a mud or sandy bottom will probably contain crab. They can also be found along the edges of river mouths. To prevent being swept away, crab need loose bottom material to burrow into during strong tidal changes. Crab are particularly fond of eel grass. It provides cover for them to hide, and to sneaking up on food.

When tides are changing rapidly, creating strong currents, crab become dormant, buried below the bottom surface or backed up against a piling or other bottom structure. As the currents ease, they come out of hiding with their appetites raging. That's why the best crabbing times are an hour before or an hour after a slack tide, high slack being best. (Slack tide is that time when the tide is at its lowest or highest point, and the tide is neither going in or out.)

Dungeness Crab *(Cancer magister)* are the favorite species. They can be found from Cook Inlet, Alaska, to the Southwest coast of Baja Mexico. In Washington State they are mainly found north of Tacoma, throughout Hood Canal, and along the coast. In Oregon and California, they are also found in the mouth of rivers. They range to depths of 750 feet. The meat is flavorful and they can grow up to ten inches across.

Because crab are enclosed in a rigid exterior skeleton, they can grow only by shedding their shells. They molt up to seven times during the first year and at a decelerating rate in subsequent years, but each is on its own cycle. Some can be soft in a particular harbor at any time of the year. A size of four inches is reached in two years, and a mature size of five and three-quarter inches in three years. Males continue growing rapidly after maturity, unlike females, and can add as much as an inch in size and may double it's weight with each molt. Male crab mature a year or more before reaching the minimum legal size for harvesting. Females are completely protected from legal harvest. With large females producing up to two and a half million eggs each winter, there is no fear of over-harvesting the resource under present regulations. Crab can live ten years or more.

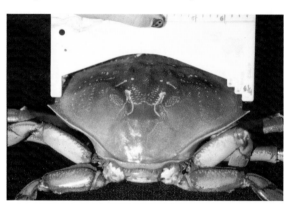

Minimum size requirements are measured across the back shell inside the outer points.

Dungeness Crabs have a purple-tinged, orange-brown shell with white-tipped claws and usually reach six to seven inches across the back. Dungeness Crab move about in "migration clusters," usually moving from deep water to shallow during the first six months of the year. The coastal specimens have a tendency to travel north. When they travel, the females remain separate from the males. If you are catching only females, it usually helps to move a hundred yards and see whether you begin catching all males. Some crab really pack their bags and move out. One, tagged and released off Westport, Washington, was captured more than eighty miles south, at Tillamook Bay, Oregon. Oregon tagged crabs have traveled from Tillamook Bay northward to Willapa Bay, Washington.

With a keen sense of smell and poor eyesight, these eight-legged creatures prefer to sit and wait for food to come to them. That's why divers will find them protecting their "territory" at the base of rocks or pilings. The biggest specimens will have hollowed out impressions and become very aggressive if anything comes too near. That's why I instruct people to lower a trap directly next to a dock, rather then throwing it out as far as they can, as so many do.

WHY ARE ALL THE CRAB DYING?

During summer months, state fisheries' departments will routinely receive calls that huge numbers of crab have died. When crab shed their shells during molting, they completely back out of the old skeleton, leaving the impression that the remains are a dead crab. So the answer is, they are not dying but simply putting on a new spring-summer wardrobe, in what has to be one of nature's most interesting phenomena.

When they move, they can be very quick, moving sideways in a true "crab-like" motion. I dropped a food morsel into a lagoon one day, and watched a sculpin (bullhead fish) and a crab race for it. They were both about 30 feet away in different directions. The crab got the food first! Let's look at the food they like best:

BAITS: The main thing to remember is that crab like "fresh" food. There's an old wives tale that crab like rotten bait. WRONG! Their favorite culinary delights are, in this order: clam meat, filleted fish carcasses (not just heads), chicken, turkey and beef. But all must be fresh! Your freezer-burned offerings will be accepted, but if you put a freezer-burned piece of fish in a trap next to a trap baited with the same type of fresh fish, you will see better results with the fresh item. Clams are natural crab food, so putting the effort to gather some large varieties (Horse, Eastern Softshell or large Butters) can lead to productive crab fishing. Smash the clam shells first, to promote a scent trail. I researched this extensively when I was developing a new crab bait for retail sale. I tried fish, chicken, and turkey alone, and combined with various other substances. The absolutely best concoction consisted of equal amounts of fresh ground salmon carcass, after filleting (bottom fish works as well), mixed with fresh ground chicken necks and backs.

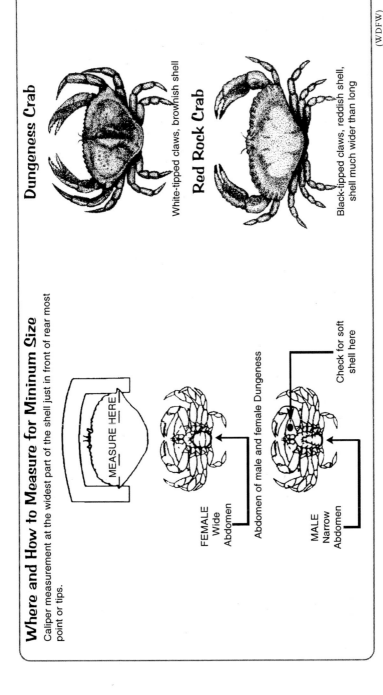

Dungeness Crab — White-tipped claws, brownish shell

Red Rock Crab — Black-tipped claws, reddish shell, shell much wider than long

Where and How to Measure for Minimum Size
Caliper measurement at the widest part of the shell just in front of rear most point or tips.

MEASURE HERE

FEMALE Wide Abdomen

Abdomen of male and female Dungeness

MALE Narrow Abdomen

Check for soft shell here

(WDFW)

The Life Cycle of a Crab
From Egg to Adult

Note that baby crabs look more like baby shrimp. Baby crabs look so different from adults that scientists once thought they were a different animal.

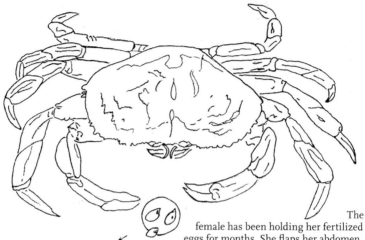

The female has been holding her fertilized eggs for months. She flaps her abdomen to release larvae, hatching from 1 to 2 million eggs, each egg about the size of a grain of salt.

As the larvae shed the egg membrane, their spines harden to discourage predators from eating them. Salmon in net pens sometimes get these spiny larvae in their gills, contributing to fish kills.

In a brief prelarval stage, the prezoea drift out from the shore eating plankton.

The crab begins to develop its 10 legs as it drifts back into shallow water. Its mavillipeds help it swim, something adult Dungeness crabs don't do well

The juvenile crab is essentially a shrimp with a small abdomen folded tightly beneath its body. From now on the crab will molt its shell several times as it grows. Each growth step is called an instar.

The larvae develop into a shrimp-like creature called a megaliops. At this stage the crab is about the size of a large mosquito. Schools of megalops seek out appropriate habitat close to shore.

CRABBING THE OREGON COAST

Along the Oregon coast, nearly all crabbing is done from jetties at the mouths of rivers. Unfortunately, there is a large number of seals and sea lions along the coast. Since the preferred type of trap is a ring, which stays put in the river currents better then a pot, the sea mammals can get directly to the bait used, competing with the crab for it.

Enter the Idaho mink rancher. This mink rancher had a problem disposing of his mink carcasses each year, until he discovered crab like this flavor while sea mammals are repelled by it. So each spring he packs up all his frozen mink carcasses, loads them in a refrigerated 18 wheeler, and sells them up and down the Oregon coast. Buy and use them while they last.

This I did with a commercial meat grinder, dropping equal portions into the vat. The fish provided the flavor of preference, and the chicken carried the flavor into the currents with an oily, long lasting texture.

HOW AND WHERE? A completely enclosed crab trap is called a "pot," and traps that lie completely flat on the bottom are called "ring traps" or "star traps." The best pots are round ones. Because square crab pots have corners, a sideways walking crab encountering a corner will likely just keep on moving away from the trap, never finding the door. If you use a round trap, the sideways traveler will keep going around the trap until it finds the door. All pots must be equipped with a means for escape if the pot is lost. Otherwise it could continue to "fish" for a long time, killing everything that gets trapped. There must be an escape opening protected by untreated cotton cord, and the access lid must be

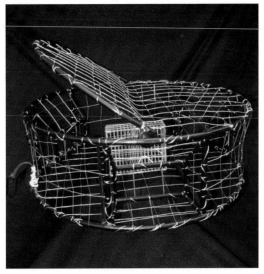

Hoop Trap for Dock Crabbing

The preferred rig for dock crabbing has two hoops with collapsible mesh netting between them. Tie line onto edge of dock and drop baited trap over the side. Trap will lie flat on bottom. Jerk up quickly every 10 to 15 minutes. Remember to tie bait securely to bottom of mesh panel.

Basket Type Crab Trap

All buoys must have (one) name, address and date clearly written upon them. Buoys must be constructed of durable material (no bleach, anitfreeze, or detergent bottles, no paint cans, etc.). Buoys must be visible on the surface at all times except during extreme tidal conditions. To indicate a crab trap, the buoy should be half red and half white, with both colors visible when in a floating position.

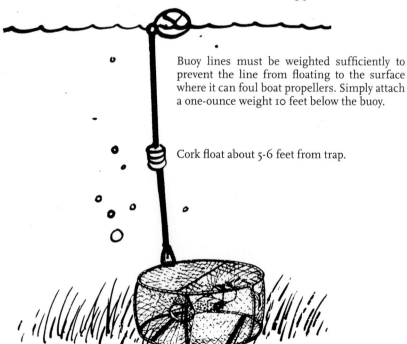

Buoy lines must be weighted sufficiently to prevent the line from floating to the surface where it can foul boat propellers. Simply attach a one-ounce weight 10 feet below the buoy.

Cork float about 5-6 feet from trap.

secured with the same cotton cord. If the pot is lost, in a few days the cord will rot away and anything inside can get out.

Your choice of fresh bait should be secured in the center of your selected trap either in a bait box, or, as I prefer, in a bait bag. A bag holds larger odd shaped pieces of bait, and allows the crustaceans a more direct access to their food. This will hold their attention better, giving the fisherman better odds of catching them, especially in a ring or star trap. A crab's claws are made for crunching, not cutting, so they cannot cut through a mesh bag.

Ring traps are legal for all areas. Secure bait in center of small ring.

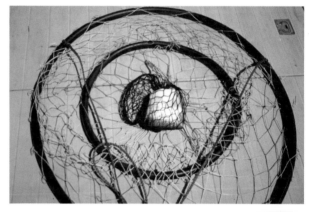

Bait "boxes" are fine, but bait "bags" work better. Bait must be fresh.

When fishing from a dock or jetty, no identification is required for the trap, but a shellfish license is required for the fisherman. When deploying traps from a boat in Washington waters, a red and white float must be attached to your line. Each buoy must have the angler's name and address. There must be a 1-ounce weight attached to the line ten feet below the buoy to prevent entangling the line in boat propellers, unless you use a leaded sinking line. Be sure to use enough line to reach bottom with enough left over to allow for incoming tide and currents. Most recreational crabbing is done in sixty feet of water or less, but commercial pots can be found in waters as deep as 400 feet. I suggest sportsmen use pot pullers on their boats. Don't hesitate to fish for crab to depths of 300 feet. Most times that is where the largest crab will be found, and in late seasons, that may be the ONLY place to find them.

DON'T PASS OFFSHORE OPPORTUNITIES: Some of the best Dungeness crab fishing in West Coast states can be found offshore. For example, in Washington, 8 million pounds are caught annually within Puget Sound, while 28 to 35 million pounds are taken from the coast. Safety is the keyword here. Although it's not necessary to go far offshore—usually just outside a breakwater or jetty, and always in less then 100 feet of water—a good boat is mandatory. I'm not talking about a "lake-boat" either. No car-toppers allowed! Eighteen to twenty- foot minimums with twin engines, and then only on good weather and tide days. The results will be rewarding. The sandy bottoms just outside the surf are perfect for crab, bottom dwelling fish and salmon when in season. Mixed bag catches are normal.

The use of a pot pulling system is nearly a necessity for retrieving heavily laden crab and shrimp pots from great depths. From a simple swinging davit, with an open block utilizing "Armstrong power", to the latest 12 volt powered units that can be operated using only your fingertips, a puller will make your boating outing much more enjoyable. And more enjoyment translates to doing it more often.

CAUTION: Gas powered pullers can be dangerous and difficult to use. The capstan bolted to the crankshaft of a small gas engine spins at 350 RPM at idle. When wrapping a retrieval line around it, backlashes happen, which can instantly pull hands through. Each year fingers are severed in this manner. Further concerns with gas powered units include the danger of carrying spare gas containers aboard, with the fire hazards involved; the obnoxious noise and fumes omitted when operating; the effects of saltwater environments on gas motor ignitions making them hard to start; and problems with winter storage that can lead to the need to rebuild carburetors each spring. Electric pullers are far safer, quieter and maintenance free, well worth any extra cost.

I always lay my traps in a line to make them easier to locate, and also to combine scent trails from each. If there is commercial gear in the area, I will lay mine near them to take advantage of the combined bait scents. When doing this, however, I always keep my floats in sight.

There was a time when I deployed a couple pots just outside the Westport Harbor breakwater in Greys Harbor next to some commercial pots. When I returned a couple hours later, I noticed the commercial gear had been removed. When I pulled my pots, I was first surprised to see my baits had not been touched. Then I was further surprised to find all my trap doors had been tied shut. I was thankful the commercial fisherman had respectfully left my pots, but I got the message that he didn't want my company.

Remember, female and male crab migrate separately. If you catch mostly female, move a hundred yards and increase the odds of catching males.

The female abdomen flap (top crab) is wide compared to the narrow male abdomen flap

There are no float color regulations in California, Oregon or British Columbia, but in Washington a half-red and half-white one must be used with crab tackle, and a yellow float must be used with shrimp tackle. Here is good insurance against sinking a float during strong currents: use three of them tied several feet apart, with the last on a weighted flag staff for ease of location. The flag staff also makes it easy to pull alongside and grab it— very important on windy days.

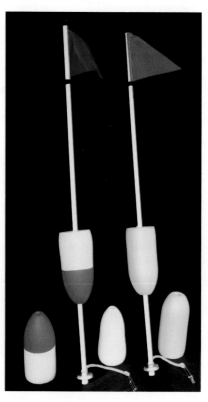

Red and white floats: Crab
Yellow floats: Shrimp

Pots can be left unattended for long periods, but rings must be "worked." Lower your ring straight down, making sure the bait stays in the center. Pull quickly every 10 to 15 minutes. When working rings from a boat, it is important to pick them up *with* the current, to maintain rope pressure. If you pick up the float and move against the current, you will likely move the small ring before lifting the outer ring, allowing the quarry to escape. When working from a dock, remember crab are very territorial and will "own" a particular piling. Larger ones dig out depressions around piling bases. Lower your ring straight down near the pilings. If you catch a big crab by the piling, usually another will quickly seize the spot. It's not good to throw a ring trap. The small ring with bait attached may land outside the large ring and you won't catch the crab that is sitting outside the trap eating your bait.

Remove your legal keepers but leave a couple small ones in your ring or pot, and gently lower back to the bottom. The little ones will go right back to eating. They won't eat your bait very fast, but will make a clacking sound that will draw additional large crabs. Some folks will even secure a small strobe light with the bait, to further attract diners. Crab respond to smell, light, and sound.

Each state's coastline, bays, and sounds have public docks, piers, and jetties where crab can be caught. Many are handicapped accessible. Most ferry landings have a public fishing area. Remember to stay off railroad trestles. They are illegal and dangerous places to be caught.

YOUR CATCH: Be familiar with the local catch regulations before beginning your outing. Different areas around each state have different size and bag limits per species, plus set fishing times and dates.

Legal sizes for male Dungeness vary from 5-3/4-inches in Oregon, to 6-1/4 inches in Washington, and 165 mm (6-1/2 inches) in British Columbia. Either sex of Red Rock crab can be collected in most areas, but only male Dungeness may be kept.

Softshell, or molting crab, can be identified by pressing the largest section of any walking leg. The section should be firm and full of meat.

Check for soft-shell "molting" condition by squeezing the leg sections. They should be firm rather than soft as this one is.

During molting the section will be soft, containing very little meat, not much flavor, and it will cost you a substantial fine if you're caught with one.

When handling any crab to be released, but especially ones in "soft" condition, handle them GENTLY! Care must be taken not to break off legs, especially claws. That can lead to their dying from bleeding to death. NEVER throw them! The impact with the water can damage even a hard crab internally. If they are holding onto the trap with a vice-grip-like claw, just wait until they relax and release their grip. When inspecting them on dock or deck, lay them on their back for control. Hold them from the bottom, with your thumb on the underside, fingers on the back. This way they cannot reach you with the powerful claws.

Red Rock crab *(Cancer productus)* have heavy, brick-red shells and black-tipped claws. They are smaller than Dungeness crab, rarely larger then six inches in shell width. They are found throughout Puget Sound and prefer rocky bottoms with little silt, often hidden under rocks or partly buried under gravel or mud. They range to depths of 260 feet.

After you have determined the proper sex and species of your catch—and it's large enough and firm—you may retain it in an empty container. Do NOT fill it with water. The inhabitants will quickly exhaust the oxygen in the water and actually drown. They simply need to be kept cool and damp. Cover them with a damp gunnysack and keep them out of the sun. If you are going to be holding them for more then a couple hours you can occasionally cover them with seawater to revive them, but don't let them stay covered more then a few minutes. Never put them on, or cover them with, ice. They may freeze, or they may drink the melting fresh water and die.

Crab should always be cooked alive (more on that later) to prevent toxins from deceased organs contaminating the meat. They can be kept alive overnight by wrapping them in wet material or newspapers and placing them in the refrigerator. Do not allow the material to dry out. They will become dormant overnight, and you can tell if they are still alive in the morning by tweaking a "feeler" and watching for eye movement. They can be temporarily revitalized by immersing in cold water.

COOKING: The best means of cooking crab is to clean them first. Some folks feel it is more "humane" that way, but the most important reason is to prevent contaminating the meat with any undesirable elements remaining on the shell or in the inedible internal organs. Most specimens will be caught with bottom muck and slime covering them, stuff we don't want to cook into our succulent meat. It is also much less messy, less smelly, and you can get much more into your cooking pot.

See the following photo series on how to clean before cooking:

To clean crab before cooking, lay the crab on its back. Place the cutting edge of a sharp knife against the shell and strike it with just enough force to crack the shell at the upper edge.

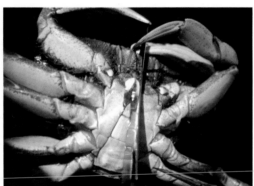

The crab will be stunned, and will offer no further resistance.

Remove the abdomen flap.

If you are still on the water, retain the flap for proof of sex.

Grasp all the legs and claw on one side with one hand, and the legs and claw on the other side with the other hand.

Fold both halves together,

and . . .

. . . remove the back.

If you are still
on the water,
retain the back
for proof of
legal size.

Remove the
gills and
discard.

Remove the
loose shell
fragments and
entrails.

Rinse the remaining bits of intestinal matter by vigorously sloshing in water.

Here is your cleaned crab half, ready to cook. This is much more sanitary than cooking the crab whole, and you can put more crabs in the same size pot.

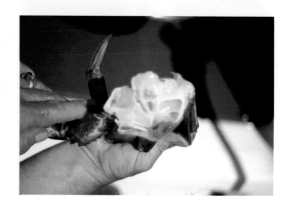

One cup of rock salt per gallon of fresh water closely simulates the salinity of natural saltwater. Add garlic powder to taste to the cooking water.

Bring water to full boil, add crab halves, return to boil. Cook 15-18 minutes

Have a cold water slush ready to receive cooked crab in order to quickly stop the cooking.

If cooked in fresh water, the meat will be very white and the flavor quite bland. It is best if they are cooked in the same water in which they are caught, if that water is clean. Fresh water can meet the salinity of natural saltwater if one cup of rock salt is added per gallon. I like to add a touch or two of garlic powder to my cooking water. There are many types of crab and shrimp boil ingredients preferred by some. See the "recipes" section of this book for suggestions. Bring the water to a boil and add your cleaned crab sections. When the water returns to a boil, time the cooking for 15 to 18 minutes. To quickly stop the cooking process, have a cold water bath ready in which to place the cooked sections. This step is unnecessary if you will be serving the sections immediately.

EATING: Hot crab meat is wonderful coming from the cooker. Pick the meat from the shell and dip it in drawn butter with another touch or two of garlic powder added. If you are going to use the crab in a salad, cool it in the icy slush solution first.

The Final Reward:
The greatest reward in crabbing is sitting around the dining table with family and friends, eating succulent crab with your fingers,and enjoying good conversation.

GREEN CRABS:
WARNING! ALIEN MONSTERS ARE COMING!

There are alien invaders headed this way that may wipe out all Dungeness crabs! *Carcinus maenas,* more commonly known as "green crab," are mean and nasty and eat everything they can catch. They are particularly fond of other shellfish, especially other crabs.

On the east coast they have been wiping out the scallop industry. The town of Edgarton, Massachusetts, located on the island of Martha's Vineyard, offered a bounty of 40 cents a pound on green crab to help save the scallops. During the first five weeks, over 15,000 pounds were caught. In Maine they wiped out all the soft shell clams.

Green crab now threaten the West Coast. First discovered in San Francisco Bay in 1991, they now range from Monterey Bay all the way to Vancouver Island, British Columbia. They will certainly enter Puget Sound, with no way to stop them.

Originally from the Far East and Asia, these hearty crustaceans, considered an "aquatic invasive species", travel around the earth in the water ballast tanks of large ships, and are deposited when the tanks are pumped out in harbors. They then migrate as the female produces eggs two million at a time. The eggs simply float out on the ocean currents. Scientists have tracked their movement at as much as five miles per day.

Legislation titled "National Invasive Species Act" has set guidelines to regulate the discharge of ballast water from ships nationwide. This is a good law, but too late. The crab are established here and are eating their way up the West Coast.

Green Crab feed on many organisms including clams, oysters, mussels, marine worms and small creatures. One adult can eat 40 half-inch clams per day and can devour crabs as large as itself.

When the Oregon Department of Fish and Wildlife issued a bulletin asking crab anglers to keep and turn in all green crab they caught, people began bringing in hundreds of other species of crab, anything they saw with a green tint. Spider Crab, Hermit Crab and many three-inch Dungeness Crab were being killed, prompting the department to rescind their request.

It was obvious that an eager but uneducated public wanted to help, but not all crab with a greenish tint are the evil aliens; in fact not all green crab are "green". The only sure way to distinguish a green crab from all other west coast crab are the five "teeth," or spikes, on either side of the front edge of the carapace, or shell. Colors may vary during molting cycles from green to orange to red. Maximum size rarely exceeds three inches.

If you are positive that your catch is a real green crab, don't return it to the water. Keep it, and report it to your department of fisheries. (Note: they can only be transported legally, dead, in a sealed container.) These crab are a real menace and must be controlled somehow, but not by randomly killing thousands of other small species of crab.

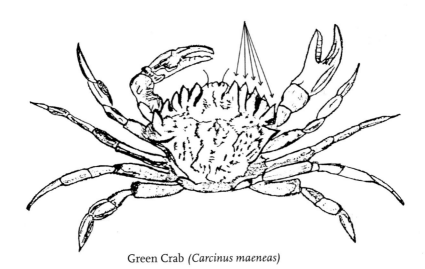

Green Crab *(Carcinus maeneas)*

The Green Crab is NOT always green.

The color varies and juveniles change color to match their surroundings.

Adults can measure 3 to 4 inches and are usually a darker green with yellow markings and the underside may be bright yellow or red.

The only true distinction between these deadly invaders and every other West Coast crab species is the five "spines" on either side of the leading edge of their shell.

Puget Sound Recreational Only, Non-Commercial & Limited Commercial Dungeness Crab Fishing Areas

The areas designated on the following three pages will usually produce the best crab fishing opportunities for the sport fisher.

The areas marked by ████ are open to recreational-only harvest during open seasons, and closed to all commercial harvest year round. Those are the best to target, and many can be accessed without a boat.

Those areas marked by blue ████ are open for sport fishers during open seasons, but have limited access for commercial fishing November 1 through February 28.

Pink ████ denotes areas that are primarily recreational, with limited commercial entry between October 15 and March 14.

The red ████ areas maybe entered by sports fishers during open seasons, along with tribal commercial fishers, but they are off limits to non-tribal commercial activity at all times.

PLEASE NOTE: All these areas are subject to review each year, and new areas might be added. For current regulations, check the Shellfish Hotline: (360) 796-4601, Ext. 320.

To enter your input about these areas or to suggest others for consideration, call the Mill Creek Regional Office at (425) 775-1331, or the Point Whitney Shellfish Lab at (360) 796-4601.

Dungeness Crab Fishing Areas:
San Juan Islands

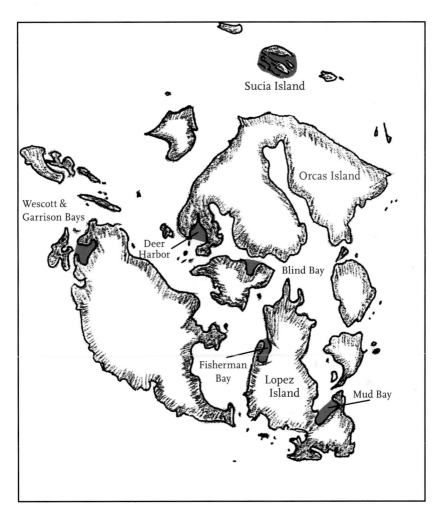

Sucia Island

Orcas Island

Wescott &
Garrison Bays

Deer
Harbor

Blind Bay

Fisherman
Bay

Lopez
Island

Mud Bay

Non-commercial Zone
Recreational All Year

Limited Commercial Oct. 15 - Mar. 14
Recreational All Year

Limited Commercial Nov. 1 - Feb. 28
Recreational All Year

Tribal Exclusive
Recreational All Year

Dungeness Crab Fishing Areas:
Padilla & Fidalgo Bays,
North to Birch Bay

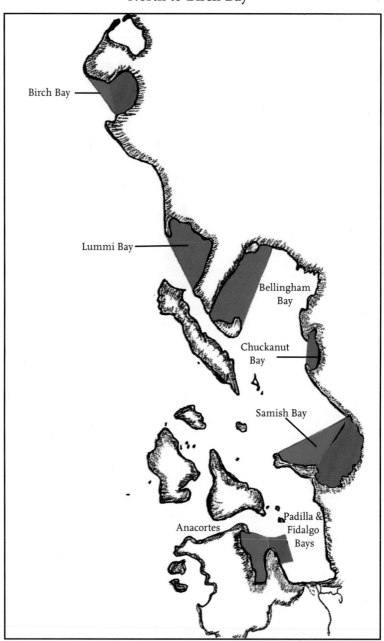

Birch Bay

Lummi Bay

Bellingham Bay

Chuckanut Bay

Samish Bay

Padilla & Fidalgo Bays

Anacortes

Dungeness Crab Fishing Areas:
Possession Point, North to
North Skagit & Similk Bays

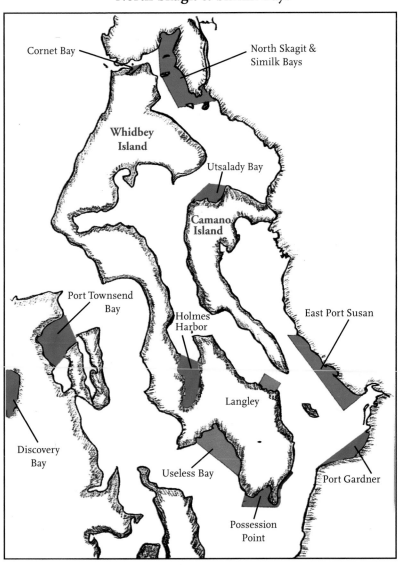

Cornet Bay

North Skagit & Similk Bays

Whidbey Island

Utsalady Bay

Camano Island

Port Townsend Bay

Holmes Harbor

East Port Susan

Langley

Discovery Bay

Useless Bay

Port Gardner

Possession Point

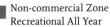 Non-commercial Zone
Recreational All Year

Limited Commercial Oct. 15 - Mar. 14
Recreational All Year

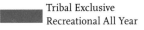 Limited Commercial Nov. 1 - Feb. 28
Recreational All Year

Tribal Exclusive
Recreational All Year

LET'S EAT SOME BAIT

Crayfish, also known as crawfish or crawdad, are not only great bass bait but are excellent table fare. Related to lobster, they are found throughout North America and most countries around the world. Crayfish are characterized by a joined head, or midsection, and a segmented body, which is sandy yellow, green, or dark brown in color. The head has a sharp snout, with the eyes on movable stalks. Crayfish are usually about 7.5 cm (3 inches) long. They have a hard outside skeleton. This jointed exoskeleton provides protection and allows movement, but limits growth. As a result, the crayfish regularly gets too big for its skeleton, sheds it, and grows a new larger one. This is called molting, and occurs six to ten times during the first year of rapid growth, but less often during the second year. For a few days following each molt, crayfish have a soft exoskeleton and are more vulnerable to predators.

I found a statistic which claimed there are more crayfish caught annually then all other shellfish combined. Why? Because there are more crayfish areas to harvest. Nearly all live in fresh water but a few survive in saltwater. They are found in nearly every pond, lake, river, stream or creek around you. Although they live at the bottom of the food chain, being eaten by fish, turtles, beavers, birds and even alligators, populations are growing at an alarming rate. Fish and game departments in several states are aware of the threat crayfish impose upon habitat in game-fish waters.

Crayfish are greedy eaters. It is a misconception that they are vegetarians. It is true that they will eat plant life and algae, but their primary diet is any live fish they can catch, plus fish eggs, worms, snails, insect larvae and bugs. This puts them in direct competition with the fish for the same foods. It is amazing how adept crayfish are at hunting during the daylight. Night time gives the them an additional huge advantage. They will strike from above, pouncing like coyotes, and stalk fish like cats stalking a bird. They have been seen eating six inch trout they have caught. With the explosive populations of crayfish all across the country, it's easy to see them wiping out game fish in many areas by competing for food and eating young fish.

Unlike other species of shellfish, you can't just throw in a trap and expect to catch them. They are very wary. Being at risk from all other predators, they feed primarily at night and although being voracious feeders, they are also very picky.

BAITS: FRESH is the main ingredient. These hard-shelled shrimp-like crustaceans are attracted to only the freshest food. Fish heads offer little meat, so fish guts and body meat are better offerings. Keep your bait frozen until ready to use. Any type of oily fish is good: salmon, herring, shad, cod, even carp, but NOT catfish, bullhead, or any type of fowl, beef, pork, dog or cat food.

Use a bait box or bait bag rather then a bait jar. You want to get and keep the attention of your prey. These critters are huge eaters so use plenty of bait. One pound in a bait box is about right for a large trap. Most bait box designs will fit in a gallon freezer bag for cleanliness. Placement of the bait depends upon the design of the trap used. There are hundreds of trap designs since crayfish are found in so many areas. Usually the bait must be secured in the center of the trap.

WHERE: Because crayfish fall at the bottom of the food chain, they need plenty of hiding places. Place your trap near a structure, like the large rip-rap boulders used to shore up river or lake banks, or near natural rock slides. You can also place them around logs or roots, pilings and docks. Not only do these areas provide cover and hiding places for them while hunting for fish, but the algae growing there provides their base food. Underwater grasses and thriving weeds are hiding cover but not good holding spots. They may jam trap entrances. Topwater cover such as lilypads are good for bass and therefore bad for crayfish. Even ponds with no fish can be loaded with crayfish: just place your trap in the deepest spot, which would give them the most protection from air breathing predators.

WHEN: Night time! Night gives crayfish a huge advantage in catching fish, therefore that is when they are most active. They are adept hunters during daylight hours, but cloudy days are better than sunny days. Only small, young ones venture out on bright sunny days.

As of this writing, no license is needed to fish for crayfish in Washington State, but there is a season from May 1 till October 31. Always check local regulations before venturing out with trap in hand.

PREPARATION: Most recipes begin with boiling. Use enough water to cover the crawfish. Use 1/2 cup of rock salt and 1/2 cup of sugar per gallon of water. Bring solution to a boil, add crawfish and boil 10 minutes, then soak for up to a half hour, checking occasionally for salt content. There are many varieties of crab-shrimp-crawfish boil packets available usually containing salt, cayenne pepper, Tabasco sauce, garlic, cloves and bay leaves. An example recipe for a boiling packet that can be used for all shellfish is one popular in Louisiana. It includes:

4 Tablespoon yellow mustard seeds
3 Tablespoon coriander seeds
2 Tablespoon whole allspice
2 Tablespoon dill seeds
1 Tablespoon crushed red pepper
1 Teaspoon whole cloves
8 Bay leaves
Salt and pepper to taste

Combine all dry ingredients thoroughly. Place in a square of muslin or cheesecloth and tie securely with string, like a large *sachet d'épices*. Add salt and cayenne or hot sauce to the water to taste, then bring to a boil.

Serve with melted garlic butter or see other recipes in this book.

MUSSELS

Mussels are like bass to my family. I grew up thinking of bass as the garbage fish that plagued us when trout fishing. If we caught one, we would drop-kick it off into the bushes so it could not reproduce. After all, what were they good for? They were scaly, bony, and too little to mess with, anyhow. You see, we didn't have the right lures to catch the bigger ones. We probably didn't know bigger ones even existed.

Mussels have become a delicacy enjoyed in the finest of restaurants. This Italian dish, *Cozze ala Arancione,* was prepared by Chef Dave Nelson. Recipe is on page 101.

Photo by Barry Gregg

Not until the early 60's, when military men from the South were transferred to Washington, did we discover the value of local bass. Those good old boys knew a good bass fight when they saw one. Washington bass angling exploded!

Mussels were like that. They always grew everywhere, on pilings and the under-sides of docks. They could cover an entire rocky beach. At low tide they were a nuisance, making it difficult to walk from water to land, when landing your rowboat.

Although we would occasionally pick one or two out for bottomfish bait when there were no piling worms about, eating one was out of the question! Anyone knew that if you ate one from a piling it would taste like the preservative used to protect the wood. If it came from the beach it would be full of grit and taste like mud, as worthless as a bass!

Only about twenty years ago did we discover what wonderful table fare these morsels could be. Although mussels had traditionally been considered a delicacy in continental Europe, we Yankees were too dumb to try eating any that might have grown in a clean environment. Although they were profuse in our marine habitat, the truth about their great flavor remained a secret. Perhaps it was intentionally kept a secret by those who knew and gathered the best for themselves; but now the secret is out. Mussels are truly a delicacy.

They thrive in saltwater, even in places where it's diluted with fresh water, such as the mouths of rivers. They grow in quiet bays and inlets, and can endure fairly high water temperatures. For these reasons, special care must be taken when harvesting. Calm harbors can accumulate high concentrations of pollutants which are not flushed out regularly. The warm waters can produce algae blooms, leading to red tide conditions.

If you find mussels growing on clean rocks, away from sand or mud, in clean cold water which has plenty of tidal flow, you could be in for a taste treat. Remember, make sure you're not on a private beach.

Blue Mussels, also known as Bay Mussels or Mediterranean Mussels, are the best. They are widely eaten in Europe, and are prolific along the west coast from Oregon to British Columbia. The only mussel species found in the Strait of Georgia, Blues will grow to a maximum length of two inches in a little over a year. Commonly found growing in clusters, the shells are oblong, blue-black or brown in color, filled with a cream or light orange meat.

Mussels (*Mytilus trossulus*, *Mytilus edulis*, and *Mytilus galloprovencilis*) have oblong, blue-black or brown shells and are usually found in dense mats attached by fine threads

Another common mussel, found only along the open coastline where the water salinity is higher, is the California Mussel, *Mytilus californianus*. It can grow to a length often inches. Its meat is orange or reddish in color. Its shell is black, and you will notice it peeling as it dries in the air between tides. These are NOT culinary delights!

Commercial shellfish farms grow their mussels attached to fiber ropes connected to long lines and rafts. This way, the mussels never touch bottom where their flavor could be contaminated by mud. They will also be free of sand, mud or grit. Consider this when gathering your own: they need to be clean.

TIP: Mussels must be kept alive until time to cook. Keep them cool and damp. If possible, keep them in a bag suspended in saltwater. This will also "purge" them, allowing them to naturally flush out sand. A better way to purge them is to place them in a bucket of saltwater and throw in a handful of corn meal. They will take in the meal while expelling their grit. The shell will be normally closed as long as they are alive, or will quickly close when touched. Before cooking discard any that do not close, as this signifies the mussel is no longer alive. After cooking, the shell should be open. Discard any still closed after cooking.

Mussels spawn during spring months, and their meat becomes thin and watery. Since the flavor dissipates too, consider mussels off the menu from January first until June. They are a "seven month delicacy," just right for summer cruising and beach combing.

HOW TO EAT: If you have gathered your mussels from unpolluted waters with no red tide warnings posted, you are ready to eat. (See the red tide information on pages 82-83.

Most folks can eat about a pound of in-shell mussels per person. Maximum limits vary between states and countries, but they are very liberal: 10 pounds per person in Washington; no limit in some areas of B.C. Always refer to current regulations for the locality you're in.

There is no reason to gather more than can be used for one meal, as they will be plentiful at the next low tide and they do not store well. Keep them cool and moist, covered with a wet sack or even seaweed.

In preparation for eating, you must first get rid of their "beards." No, they don't need a shave before dinner like Uncle Ralph. They have whisker-like fibers at the shell hinge, which they use to attach to their home site. These will come off easily as you scrub the shells with a stiff brush.

Now they are ready for cooking in a variety of ways. The easiest and first step in most recipes is to put just enough water in a pan to cover the bottom, and add the mussels. Cover with a loose lid and bring the water to a boil, steaming the mussels until the shells open. After steaming, discard any shells that didn't open.

At this point the meat can be scooped out of the shells and eaten as you would steamed clams. Because their flavors are complementary, mussels and clams can be prepared together in this manner and served with melted butter.

OYSTERS

The west coast of the United States and British Columbia is awash with oyster beds containing the world's best tasting specimens. Numerous oyster companies process and ship more than two million gallons, or well over eight million tons, annually of shucked samples of these wonderful morsels to restaurants around the world. They become menu items, satisfying discriminating palates in the form of Oysters Rockefeller, oyster stew, fried oysters and in the form of other recipes found in this book.

Oysters can be the gold at the end of the rainbow for boaters, or the bounty of the beach for land lovers. But when you encounter a cluster of the shell-encased entrees fit for royalty, there are certain things one must consider.

By 1920, Washington's tide flats had been picked clean of native "Olympic Oysters" because of the tremendous demand of San Francisco restaurants, which began with the 1849 Gold Rush. Harvesting practices then did not consider how oysters reproduce.

Let's look at the life cycle of oysters, so we will know better how to find them and how to protect their communities.

Oysters are bisexual. They all begin life as males. After about four years they become female for the first time. Thereafter, they alternate between producing eggs and sperm. Occasionally one can be found nurturing both eggs and sperm. Usually, an oyster is in one cycle or the other.

In the summer something within an oyster causes it to become sexually aroused. It surely has to do with the sun high overhead at just the right angle, and the flow of summer tides which aren't too strong but just fast enough to carry eggs and sperm together and deposit them along the nearby beaches.

When conditions are just right, millions of microscopic eggs are released, triggering a response from the "males" to release gallons of sperm. When the eggs are fertilized they become "spat," also known as "seed." The spat then floats and swims, using tiny, hair-like cilia as motor power to push themselves about. An extremely high percentage of the spat will be consumed by jellyfish, starfish and other predators, or will simply float out into deep waters. After about eighteen days, the remaining spat will have grown a thin shell.

While growing the shell, the emerging sea life will produce a bit of glue. At this time it can be seen as an oyster under a microscope, and it is known as a "set." It is ready to find a home for life. It will attach itself to some firm object at or slightly below sea level during the time between high and low tide. In an environment of sunlight, sun warmth, and a cleansing tidal flow which will also supply food, the oyster will flourish. A favorite place for attaching is on other oyster shells lying on the beach. This is a reason for shucking your oysters on the beach, leaving the shells where you found them. More on that later.

The oysters immediately begin to grow, and are soon visible to the naked eye. By the first winter, the shell will have hardened, and each oyster will begin its first dormant period. During dormancy its growth

Pacific Oyster
Crassotrea gigas
Irregular, chalky-white shell. Often found in groups attached to one another or to a solid object. (WDFW)

slows, but this is also the time when mature oysters are most flavorful.

Oysters are edible during any month of the year, but their flavor and condition are best when temperatures are lowest, and the oysters are not in a spawning or growth cycle. This is also the time when the meat is fullest and firmer.

During the first four years, all oysters are in the male stage, and the majority grow to an adult size of four to five inches. After the first year, the shell becomes thicker and the meat becomes the most flavorful. "Shooters," oysters eaten raw and served on a half shell, are always two to three inches long. After an oyster reaches four inches, it is still good for frying, broiling, or other methods of cooking, but it is too large for eating raw. Really large oysters of five inches or more should be chopped up and used in stews.

WHERE TO FIND OYSTERS: There are two types of oysters along the west coast of North America: the native "Olympia" and the imported "Pacific" variety. Olympics are seldom over one and a half inches long, while any larger oysters will probably be the Pacific variety. Pacifics can grow to seven inches across.

Olympic oysters can be found in waters from California to Alaska, glued to smooth rocks and the undersides of large boulders. They are usually attached along their full length, making them very difficult to remove. It is easier to open them while they are still attached to their home rock rather than trying to remove them. But that is not an easy task either. It's hard to believe these fast growing bivalves were almost harvested into extinction in the years between 1850 and 1900.

Their small size and the difficulty of harvesting Olympic oysters prompted the importation of Pacific oysters from Japan, beginning in 1905 with a planting in Samish Bay, near Bellingham, Washington. Since then they have been introduced in Tomales Bay, Humbolt Bay, and Drakes Bay, California; along the Oregon coast; in Willapa Harbor, Greys Harbor, and throughout Puget Sound in Washington; and along the British Columbia and Southeastern Alaska shorelines. Considering their prolific reproduction and their migratory patterns of drifting with the tides, it's no surprise that oysters can be found along the entire West Coast.

The concern in harvesting oysters is that you gather them in an environmentally safe location, during the best time periods, making sure to stay on public beaches. Pacific Oysters are always found in the intertidal zone, between high and low tide levels. This is because only the surface waters are warm enough to create sets and promote their survival. If they wash into deeper water, or are discarded overboard, they can survive but will probably be eaten by starfish or other predators.

SAFE PLACES: Oysters are the water filters of the seas. They are very efficient at removing impurities from water, so you want to make sure no pollutants are being discharged near your oyster beds. Watch for sewers or septic tank outfalls, and do not collect oysters near a marina or an area of summer homes. Many times they will not have adequate sewer systems. An area where boats regularly moor can be another source of serious pollution.

I saw an extremely interesting illustration of the efficiency of oysters as water filters which was presented by the Washington Department of Fisheries. An equal amount of harmless algae was placed in three aquarium tanks, turning the water a murky green. One tank had no oysters, one had six, and the third had a dozen. Within a few hours the murkiness of the waters had dissipated according to the number of oysters present. The tank with twelve oysters was crystal clear, the one with six was clearing, but the one with no oysters was even murkier.

Constantly gathering food, a single oyster will pump more than 100 gallons of water through its shell each day! The filtering of the gills is non-selective. While removing nutritious plankton, they also separate bacteria, silt and chemicals from the water. The material ingested is a concentration of what is in the water. Biologists use oysters to sample water quality. After oysters have been placed in a bay for 24 hours, scientific examination can reveal what contaminants are present. Be careful where you gather oysters. You will be eating whatever is in the water.

SAFE TIMES: Oysters are good for eating all year, but some times are better than others. It's an old wives tale that you should not eat shellfish during months without the letter "r," but the tale points to a warning worth heeding. The months without the letter "r" are the summer months of May, June, July and August. This is when improperly stored shellfish can most easily spoil, when higher levels of pollutants may be present, and when one may encounter "red tides." Red tides occur when increased sunlight, higher water temperatures and nutrients levels combine to produce a population explosion of plankton, often turning the water brown or red. These occurrences are called "blooms" and can be highly toxic. Although not all blooms are toxic, all do affect the flavor of oysters. Never eat an oyster when a bloom is present.

Another consideration during this time of year is the spawning cycle. The water temperature must be above 50° Fahrenheit at the bed, and this usually happens in late July or August. The flavor of the meat diminishes a week or so before the oyster reproduces, and the meat is thin and watery for about three weeks after spawning.

One of the hardest decisions in gathering oysters is where to do it. When beach combing or cruising, you'll see many oyster beds during low tide. Determining which are on public beaches can be tough. Many deserted looking beaches containing oyster or clam beds are privately owned. Always look for NO TRESPASSING signs, and obey them.

So now you've found a bed of oysters that you are reasonably sure are not on private property. You have checked up and down the bay for any sources of contamination, and it's not spawning time. You are ready to partake of a culinary delight! Remember, the smaller are the better tasting, and the larger are the best spawners.

If you plan to barbecue your catch, you will need a bag or bucket for your collection. If you will be opening your treasure before cooking, it's best to do so on the beach where the oysters were found. You will need a clean bucket or a bowl with a lid. You will also need a shucking knife, and you will need a hammer, or suitable prying tool. Some places, such as Washington State, restrict the use of hammers.

If the oyster is attached to small pebbles or rocks, the whole mass can be picked up and the rocks easily knocked off. Many times several individual oysters can be gathered and separated from the same mass. If they are crowded together, they will usually be attached only at their hinges, and can easily be broken apart by gentle tapping with your tool. If they are glued flat to a big rock, they are best opened in place, since it may be impossible to dislodge them without breaking the shell.

Opening oysters, called "shucking," is difficult, but with practice it can become quite simple. There are annual oyster shucking contests where professional shuckers routinely win by opening a dozen oysters in less than one minute. The *real* art of the contest is opening them without cutting the meat. The meat of "oysters on the half-shell," which you might order in a restaurant, or those you would purchase at the supermarket, must not be damaged by a cut. Oysters damaged when opened by processors are called "cuts," and are much less valuable.

In order to open oysters without nicking the meat, we first must know what lies inside the shell. The lower half shell is usually more rounded and extends beyond the flatter upper half of the oyster. The hinge will be at the small end, with the shell opening at the larger, more rounded end. The meat will be lying in the rounded lower shell with a strong adductor muscle attached to the lower shell, and a weaker adductor muscle attached to the upper shell. These muscles are used by the oyster to keep the shell closed. One of these muscles needs to be cut cleanly to open the oyster, and then the other severed to remove the meat.

A special knife is made for this process, and it is important to use it for safety and convenience. It has a handle large enough for you to grip easily and to control the strong, stubby, rounded blade. The tip of the knife should be sharp and thin enough to slip between the lips of the shells. A heavy leather glove should be worn on the hand which will be used to hold the oyster. You can protect yourself from an inevitable slip of the knife by wearing a workman's cloth-backed leather glove. Hold the oyster in your off hand, rounded side down, and the knife in your strong hand. I find it easier to steady the oyster on a table or other firm surface with my off hand. Attack the shell from the side, about mid length. Slip the knife between shell halves and force the blade downward, under the meat, to sever the lower adductor muscle. This motion can be easily controlled by starting the blade between the shells, aiming downward, and then lifting the whole oyster a few inches off the table and slamming it back down.

Ladies to whom I've taught this method find it takes much less strength to penetrate the shell with the knife. A sweep with the blade will sever the lower muscle, allowing the shell to open. Another sweep along the upper shell will release the meat.

An easier method of opening the oyster is by baking or barbecuing just long enough to open the shell a crack. Then it can easily be opened all the way with a table knife. Whichever way you do it, you should wind up with a clean uncut morsel, ready to be eaten raw or prepared in a number of different ways.

Size should be considered when deciding how to prepare your oysters. Extra small (10 to 12 in an 8-ounce container) or small (7 to 9 per 8-ounce) can be served raw, but any larger oysters should always be cooked for the best culinary results. Medium oysters (5 or 6 per 8-ounce) are quite tasty, but should be chopped and fried or used in stews.

Since smaller means better eating, an oyster two to three inches in length will be best. These will be the extra small to small specimens. When an oyster reaches four inches or more, the internal organs become so large that the texture is impaired.

After shucking your catch, the shells should be left upon the beach from which they were gathered. The fact that the spat will be attached to them (remember this reproduction stage) is one reason to leave the shells. There is another reason: possible parasites hostile to oysters. There are a number of tiny parasites which attach themselves to oyster shells, and although they do not affect human consumption, they can be quite deadly to the oysters. One of the most common parasites, for example, is a snail-like creature called a "drill," because it can burrow through the shell and eat the contents. These parasites can be spread from contaminated beds to healthy ones through human transportation. So leave the shells where you found them.

Since oysters can be gathered only during reasonably low tides, you may want to store a few for tomorrow's dinner. They can be kept alive by keeping them cool and moist. Do not allow them to stand in water, as the oxygen will be used up and they will suffocate. They also do not like fresh water, so don't let them be rained upon. The best way is to store them in an open mesh container submerged in sea water. Hang it from a dock or your boat. Stored this way, they will last several weeks. Otherwise, keep them in the shade and covered by sea-water-moistened burlap bags. A partially opened shell indicates a dead oyster, and should be discarded. Since oysters are best when fresh, you may want to harvest only enough for one meal. Leave the rest for the next low tide expedition. Bag limits vary, but usually are 15 to 18 per day, with a two day maximum possession limit. Some area restrictions require that the oysters be opened on the beach, with shells left behind, and shellfish licenses are always required for each person. Check your local regulations.

HOW TO EAT YOUR "SHOOTERS": There are many great recipes for preparing oysters for the table. The first is the simplest and easiest. Just eat them raw. Restaurant menus will refer to this as "oysters on the half shell," or maybe "shooters." Only the smallest oyster is best eaten in this manner. The larger ones will have good flavor, but the internal organs are big enough to discourage most folks from wanting to eat them. Raw oysters should be thoroughly chewed to enjoy maximum flavor. If you swallow one whole, you miss the best flavor, and the experience is not unlike swallowing a raw egg. YUK!

Since oysters are enjoyed around the world there are recipes from everywhere. We offer several variations in the recipes section of this book. Check them out and *bon appetit.*

THE WORLD'S BEST OYSTER: Or, what's a Kumamoto? One hundred years ago, American shellfish managers discovered Japanese oyster growers were cultivating a previously unknown species in a tiny remote bay on the southernmost island of Japan, Kyushu. *Crassostrea sikamea*, now known as Kumamoto, were being grown in the bay of the same name.

The meat of these tiny oysters with a deeply cupped shell, only slightly larger than Olympia's, is beautifully plump and sweet. The Americans began importing all the Kumamotos ships could carry. Then came the big war. Immediately after the "big one" was dropped, the American growers returned to Kumamoto Bay. This time they wanted just seed. Millions of seed were planted in Humboldt Bay, California. They spread well and thrived, but soon the growers discovered that they grew too slowly to be viable on the shucked market.

Fast-forward to 1982: oysters on the half shell (shooters) were introduced to upscale restaurants in San Francisco and the race for more oysters was on. Humboldt Bay was suddenly the center of the oyster world, being overloaded with the slow growing bi-valve. The seed was worth many more times then its weight in gold,w and oyster farms from California to Washington began fighting over it.

Sadly, the Kumamoto Oyster is now extinct in Kumamoto Bay. Pollution has killed them off. It is now a rare specimen in West Coast waters, and a reminder of man's folly in the oceans.

PEARLS? When chomping your oyster on the half shell, a little care should be taken not to bite the occasional pearl. Although our west coast varieties are not known for possessing gem quality pearls, it is not uncommon to find blobs of calcium with no commercial value. These blobs are dull colored and cannot be polished to any brilliance. They are a bit of a nuisance, as they have been known to chip teeth of folks munching their shooters too fast.

SHRIMP AND PRAWNS

Some call them shrimp, but they are not merely the little guys of the seas. My family call them "San Juan Lobster." I'm here to say—whatever you call Spot Prawns (Shrimp)—they are the tastiest morsels grown in water. To put a catch of prawns in the cooking pot, it is essential to use a boat. The sea creatures we seek are going to be found in deep water, very deep water. They have been found in water up to depths of 1500 feet, but are usually caught between 200 and 400 feet. The "shrimp zone" of 40 fathoms (240 feet) is most productive.

I prefer to target the Spot Shrimp, *Pandalus platyceros,* which is considered a prawn. They grow to 10 inches long, with the meat in their tails weighing in at two ounces. That's an 8 to-the-pound tail in your

The tastiest morsel living beneath the sea is the Spot Prawn, *Pandalus platyceros,* with tail meat weighting up to 8 tail per pound. Note the large white spots on its back.

seafood market. Sidestripe Shrimp, *Pandalopsis dispar,* and Pink Shrimp, *Pandalus eous,* are the smaller cousins. They can be caught in shallow waters, even off docks, and especially at night when most shrimp species move to shallow zones. Sidestripe Shrimp will weigh-in at 20 to 30 per pound, and Pink Shrimp will tip the scales at 60 per pound. Eating them requires a lot of shell-peeling to recover the salad-size snacks.

We need to understand more about the different species in order to know how and where to catch them. Shrimp have a definite pattern of daily migration, which all sport shrimpers should keep in mind. Prawns and shrimp migrate into deep waters by day and move into shallow waters by night. Tests have shown that spot prawns concentrate in waters of 160 to 360 feet deep by day, but are found in 60 to 160 feet of water at night.

Sidestripe are the largest shrimp along the northwest coast. They are commonly found with their spot prawn cousins by night and day. Pink

Shrimp, however, are caught in trawl nets in deep water, but swim toward the surface to feed at night and during extremely overcast days. Pinks are also found 12 to 20 miles offshore, and are a major part of commercial trawl fishing.

Back in 1982, I worked 100 shrimp pots commercially in Hood Canal during the entire month of June. Those were certainly the "good old days". Anyone could have a commercial prawn license for just fifty bucks. As I remember, there were only about eight of us "white guys" plus

A nice catch of side-stripe shrimp, weighing in at 20-30 shrimp per pound.

about double that many tribal fishers. That month of June was one of the best weather months on record and was about the best month of my life. I know I ate up a good portion of my profits. Part way through it I flew my girlfriend up from California. When she found how good our Washington prawn taste, well, we've been married ever since.

In 2006, Washington State sold 228,000 shellfish licenses to sport crab fishermen, most of whom also fish for prawn. That is a far cry from the activity we saw in 1982. Due to the increase in the number of sportfishermen, this fragile resource is protected by drastically reduced open seasons. Puget Sound areas open in early May. Hood Canal opens for only four HOURS opening day; several other areas are open for only eight HOURS. Several shrimp districts do not even open, and another only opens one Wednesday. Check the regulations pamphlet closely before deciding when and where to go.

With the shortened openings, you should be prepared for "Combat Shrimping". Be efficient with your time on the water. Have your tackle prepared to deploy BEFORE leaving the dock. Best fishing time is an hour before and after each slack tide, or when the currents are slowest. The "sweet zone" for prawn, during daylight hours, is 40 fathoms (240 feet) but be ready to set gear between 180 and 320 feet. (Use at least 25% more line than depth.) With the right gear, using the best bait, at the right place and time, a license limit of prawn can be attained in just one pull. With another restriction of just four pots per boat regardless of the number of licensed individuals aboard, you can see the importance to "GIT-R-DONE", quick‼

TACKLE: I prefer to use pots with a 7/8-inch mesh opening, making them legal for use anywhere, including Washington's Hood Canal. We are only going after the big Spot Prawns, and there is less water drag when retrieving these pots than there is with finer mesh gear. Whatever size mesh you use, secure plenty of weight inside the pots—7 to 10 pounds minimum. Use plenty of line: at least 100 feet longer than the depth, or as previously mentioned, 25% more line than depth. *This is important.* It will compensate for tidal pull and wave action. Use a leaded or "sinking" line, or secure an ounce of weight 10 feet below your yellow identification buoy to keep it from floating up into somebody's propeller. That buoy must have your name and address on it.

A single 5 x 11 inch buoy will only support 8 pounds of weight. That is the weight of 300 feet of leaded (sinking) line. It will not remain on the surface with that weight in any current. If your float sinks in a tidal current you will need to be back there at a complete slack tide to retrieve it. For that reason it's best to use multiple floats several feet apart and it's useful to have the final float be on a staff, weighted on one end, with a distinguishing flag or ribbons on the upper end. Use dark colors since they are easier to find with whitecap backgrounds.

BAIT: As in so many areas, technology is changing the type of bait we use for shrimping. For many years the bait of choice has been the cheap and greasy fish-flavored cat food. Puss-n-Boots Fisherman's Platter was actually formulated for use as shrimp bait in Hood Canal. The best bait for prawn is salmon MEAT, not just heads. It may seem sacrilegious to use a salmon fillet to turn it into a few pounds of shrimp meat, but HEY, this is COMBAT FISHING! Remember the opening is measured in just HOURS? (It's amazing how fast prawn can eat a salmon filet) The next best bait is the cheapest fish flavored cat food you can find. Watch for store sales and ask about case lots. You will use a case in just a couple days of fishing. If you stick with the cat food, remove and properly stow the label to prevent littering, then perforate the can along the sides and at both ends. Shrimp and prawn traps have built in bait holders. Most will hold two cans of cat food or a sizeable portion of fish carcass. Whatever bait you use, you want the scent to disperse quickly, attracting shrimp.

A powerful new blend is being marketed in a pellet form, for use in plastic containers with small holes. Commercial shrimpers swear by this product due to its lasting powers, measured in days. The pellets, available from Canada, are favored by commercial fishermen, but they dissolve too slowly for our combat style of fishing. If you choose to try them, it's best to crunch them and mix them with shrimp oil. That's still not as good as salmon and it's more expensive.

Plastic commercial shrimp bait jars are produced with small inch diameter holes all over them. Using pellet bait with them commercially is fine as is, but they need to be modified for sport use. Connect many of the holes using a sharp knife, to increase water flow through the container. Crush the pellets and mix with shrimp oil, inexpensive fish eggs or other suitable oil creating a paste. Loosely fill the container with the paste so a scent trail will quickly form when the trap is deployed.

WHERE? 40 fathoms is the "sweet zone" for prawn, but they travel extensively. They rise off the bottom like a cloud of locust ravaging crop lands. Many times when your depthfinder shows a large "bait ball", it can be a concentration of prawn in search of your bait laden pots. Imagine them settling around your gear. "MOTHER LODE".

Placing your gear upon bottom humps, ridges or ledges is good for dispersing scent trails into currents. It is also an easy way to lose gear. I hate it when that happens. I like to set my gear in bottom bowls or canyons. A good Northern Puget Sound example is the 40 fathom canyon running along the west side of San Juan Channel, between San Juan and Lopez Islands, just inside Cattle Pass. Prawn prefer to hang out in these depressions, out of the currents and waiting for food to drop in, while hiding from predators. Remember, they are near the bottom of the food chain.

HOW? I find my spot by chart and depthfinder. My wife will be handling the boat from the flybridge. When she sees me drop the pot, she will crank into a tight ten knot circle while I deploy 300 to 400 feet of leaded sinking line through a leather gloved hand. Finally multiple floats will go over, the last a flagged float kit for easy recognition. The reason for the tight circle action is to assure the pot goes "straight" down. That's important if you are shooting for hitting a hump or ledge. If you string your gear in a straight line there is a tendency to pull the pot a bit aside and it may land tangled or upside down.

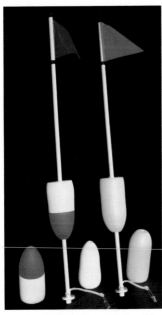

Red and white floats: Crab tackle
Yellow floats: Shrimp tackle

There are no float color regulations in California, Oregon or British Columbia, but in Washington a yellow float must be used with shrimp tackle, and a half red and white one must be used with crab tackle. To insure protection from sinking a float during strong currents, use three floats tied several feet apart, with the last on a weighted flag staff for ease of location. The flag staff also makes it easy to pull alongside and grab it. That's very important on windy days.

I'll lay the string of four pots in a straight line from shallow to deeper 50 yards apart. After soaking 30 minutes I'll pull the first for a check. If there are not many in the trap, I'll move 50 to 100 yards, at the same depth. I'll check the second pot, and so on until I find a good pot load. Then I'll concentrate there.

Using my depth finder, and during a slack tide, I'll try to set my pots about 40 fathoms deep on the high point of an underwater ridge. This is the best place for the bait to leave a scent trail. The weight you attach is important for holding onto the exposed ridge. Ten pounds of weight is not excessive, but anywhere from 7 to 15 pounds may be used. The best shrimping time is from an hour before to an hour after a slack tide, or when there is little tidal flow. During stronger tidal flows the shrimp hide behind structures for protection from being swept away. For this reason you would also want to place your gear behind some protection, or within the previous mentioned depressions.

Rules, regulations and limits vary, and in some states are very complicated. Before starting out, refer to the local shellfish regulations for the area you will be targeting. For example, Hood Canal's season is not announced until May, for a 3 to 6 day opening, Wednesdays and Saturdays only, and then only from 9 a.m. to 1 p.m., with an 80 prawn limit. I use an EZ-PULL electric puller that is so much fun to use I have a hard time just waiting for the next pull. As I've stated previously, with the best bait, gear, time and place, limits should come quickly. It's just like digging razor clams. It is so much fun, but it just doesn't last long enough.

The use of a pot pulling system is nearly a necessity for retrieving heavily laden crab and shrimp pots from great depths. From a simple swinging davit, with an open block utilizing "Armstrong power", to the latest 12 volt powered units that can be operated using only your fingertips, a puller will make your boating outing much more enjoyable. And more enjoyment translates to doing it more often.

CAUTION: Gas powered pullers can be dangerous and difficult to use. The capstan bolted to the crankshaft of a small gas engine spins at 350 RPM at idle. When wrapping a retrieval line around it, backlashes

EZ-Pull electric puller

happen, which can instantly pull hands through. Each year fingers are severed in this manner. Further concerns with gas powered units include the danger of carrying spare gas containers aboard, with the fire hazards involved; the obnoxious noise and fumes omitted when operating; the effects of the saltwater environment on gas motor ignitions making them hard to start; problems with storage during winter that can lead to the need to rebuild carburetors each spring. Electric pullers are far safer, quieter, and maintenance free—well worth the cost.

CARE & COOKING: Prawns can be kept alive nearly indefinitely in a bucket of the cold water from which they came. As the water warms and oxygen is depleted the captives will become lethargic. Just replace the water to revive them.

I prefer to remove the heads and store the tails in a ziploc bag on ice. If I'm going to freeze some I'll fill the bag with fresh water. They will freeze like that for years with no loss of flavor. Make sure there are no air pockets and don't overfill with water. Leave room for freezing expansion.

When there is no prawn size restriction the heads do not need to be kept. Some areas have size restrictions and the heads must be retained in a container while on the water. Again, check the ever changing regulations for the area you plan to fish before you go.

Popular cooking methods are boiling or sautéed in butter and garlic. Peel before sautéing but boil in shell. To boil, use the water from which they came if it's clean, or duplicate the salinity of sea water by adding one cup of rock salt to each gallon of fresh water. I like to add garlic or a "boil" mixture. Bring the water to a boil, add the shrimp, bring back to a boil and carefully time cooking for 5 to 8 minutes. Longer cooking will produce firmer texture. Remove and place in cold water to stop the cooking process. After peeling, some tails will have a dark vein of entrails, which can be easily pulled out or ignored.

These are a wonderful treat, eaten as they are, or used in a variety of hot or cold dishes. See the recipe section for preparation suggestions.

The Anatomy of a Squid

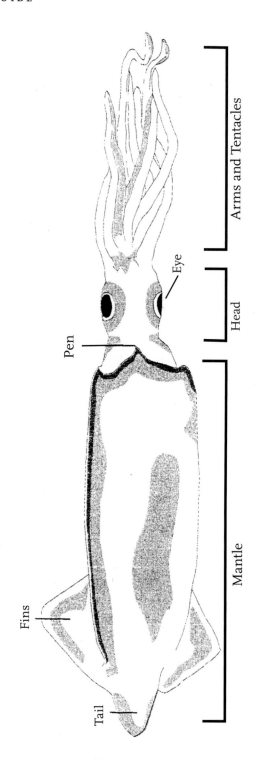

Arms and Tentacles

Eye

Head

Pen

Mantle

Fins

Tail

SCRUMPTIOUS SQUID

The good news is that we have no giant, Hollywood-type, submarine-grabbing squid in West Coast waters. The best news is that our local waters are loaded with mouth watering calamari-quality squid.

Biologically, squid belong to the class of mollusks known as cephalopods. In this class are octopus but with some definite differences in personalities. Octopus are bottom dwelling, shy and elusive, while squid are free swimming, acrobatic, schooling creatures that attract attention from fishermen and fish alike. In fact, many fishermen fish for squid just for their bait qualities.

Pacific Squid rarely grow to more then a foot in length, with the average size being 8 to ten inches. Interestingly, the larger adult sizes are found the farthest from open sea, in Southern Puget Sound and deep inside San Francisco Bay.

WHEN: Expert squid fishermen claim the schools begin showing up in near-shore waters nearest the open sea, such as Neah Bay, in May, and continue further inside through summer, fall and finally to South Sound into February.

Catching squid is exclusively a night-time adventure. The schools are attracted to light and glitter. Consequently, public piers are good squiding locations due to their usually being well lit. You can tell the schools are in when you see hardcore anglers showing up after dark, in any weather condition, towing power generators for operating bright halogen lights which are used to attract the squid to their waiting lures. The same rules apply if you decide to squid-jig from a boat near the shoreline. Please remember, however, to be a considerate sportsperson and make sure your light is not disturbing onshore residents or other navigating boaters.

Squid *(Loligo Opalescens)*

Here's how hungry squid operate. They lurk in the dark fringes near a patch of lighted water, and then lunge into the bright area after anything they think is food. Their natural favorites are young herring and other small fish.

EQUIPMENT NEEDED: All in all, squidding is one of the most inexpensive ways to get yourself a gourmet meal. You don't need a boat. You can take advantage of free public fishing piers. Another good thing is that jigging equipment is neither complicated nor costly.

Almost any style of rod and reel will work. "Light and long" is best, something that is sensitive and will telegraph slight changes. Line weight can be anything from 6 to 20 pound test, but the best sport and best chance of success come with the lighter line.

Lures vary as much as kernels of popcorn, some commercial made and some homemade, in colors from blue, pink, green, red, orange, amber to clear, but all with luminous or "glow-in-the-dark" features and/or light-gathering glitter. Remember, the idea is to attract the attention of squid lurking in the shadows to something that resembles food moving through the light.

Most lures vary in size from two to four inches, with rows of upslanted prongs. Made of various materials, the best are well weighted so they can be cast a distance or efficiently "jigged" straight up and down. Remembering that squid do not "bite" their prey, but instead lunge out of darkness to wrap their tentacles around food, they will get snagged upon the lure's upslanted prongs. Once caught, a steady retrieval is required to prevent their escape.

Artificial light can be produced from spotlights and lanterns (be careful of flame around gas containers) to generator-powered floodlights. Don't forget to take a bucket for your catch.

REGULATIONS: These vary state-to-state, so check yours locally. Most are open year around with only a shellfish license required. Washington, for example, allows year-round squidding state-wide, except closed in Hood Canal, with a daily limit of 5 quarts or 10 pounds. Oregon fishing regulations don't even mention squid, while California simply states there is no daily limit.

TWO WORDS OF CAUTION: Squid have a defense mechanism: dark ink. They shoot the ink at intruders who come too close, and on land, this could be you. In the water, it is an effective defense that creates a cloud, through which the squid makes a quick getaway. However, don't be overly upset about getting squid ink on your hands and clothes. Not surprisingly, the ink is water soluble and washes off easily if you act before it dries.

My second note of caution is a bit more sinister. It's good to remember that these creatures have a powerful and sharp parrot-like beak. They bite things like food and perceived enemies that are not alert. Again, this could be you.

PREPARING THE CATCH: There are two basic ways of cleaning squid, depending on whether your recipe calls for cutlets or strips, or requires the whole mantle or rings. The sketches and directions on the following pages describe these two methods.

Method A
This method is the faster of the two. Use if recipe calls for cutlets or strips.

Step 1: Slip knife inside mantle and slit lengthwise along underside, or belly. Open mantle and scrape away viscera and pen (transparent backbone).

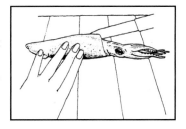

Step 2: To remove tentacles, cut in front of eyes. Squeeze tentacles near cut end to pop out hard, chitinous beak (see Inset). Discard beak, pen, head and viscera. Reserve mantle and tentacles

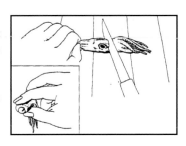

Step 3: Make cut in mantle about 1/4 inch from tail end (see Inset). Holding membrane near cut, pull mantle away from membrane. Discard membrane. Rinse mantle with cold water; Pat dry with paper towels. Use mantle whole or cut into strips widthwise. Use tentacles in recipe, or fry and serve as an appetizer.

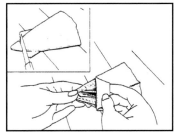

Method B
Use if recipe calls for whole mantles or rings.

Step 1: Holding mantle in one hand, pinch pen (transparent backbone) with index finger and thumb of opposite hand, separating pen from mantle.

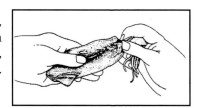

Step 2: Gently pull pen out of mantle, easing viscera out along with pen. Cut away tentacles as in Method A, Step 2.

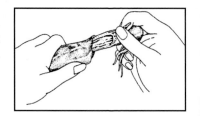

Step 3: (Not illustrated). Scrape membrane to loosen from mantle. Peel away all membrane and discard. Rinse mantle thoroughly with cold water to remove any remaining viscera. Pat dry with paper towels.

Step 4: Use mantle whole or cut into rings. Use tentacles in recipe, or fry and serve as an appetizer.

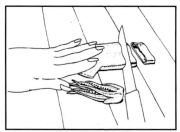

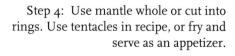

Calamari, as chefs are calling squid, is nothing new as a gourmet food. It also is nothing new as the basis for good home cooking. Cooks all over Europe and in Mediterranean and Asian nations have known the virtue for centuries. All you have to do is look at the abundance of recipes for squid and you will realize that it is well-established dining fare around the world.

There are many good things to say about calamari as a main ingredient. It is an excellent source of lean nutrition, lower in fat and calories than many other protein sources. On top of that, it is wonderfully versatile. It can be used for appetizers, soups, salads or main dishes. It can be sauteed, simmered, stir-fried or baked. I've never tried to barbecue it, but that's a possibility. It can also be pickled.

It can be used in small pieces, in strips, in rings, as a tube with stuffing or in flat filets. I know one inventive Naval officer, serving as an admiral's personal chef, who uses flat cuts of squid in place of lasagna noodles.

Squid also lends itself to many flavor personalities. There are Scandinavian, Asian, Mexican, French, Russian, Spanish, Italian and of course, American menu variations. Just rememberm, squid belong to the same food group as clams, scallops, oysters and abalone.

To best enjoy this fragile seafood, be careful of cooking times. The flesh is firm but contains very little natural juice and is delicate. Consider three minutes the maximum time for sauteing, which requires higher heat, and 20 minutes the minimum time for a stew, which calls for lower temperatures.

The same goes for marinades. Timing is important. Lacking its own juices, squid quickly absorbs marinades and their flavorings. Thirty minutes is probably the maximum soaking time.

By understanding the basics, of handling this delicate but accommodating seafood, you are likely to think of many ways to adapt it to your own recipes. For a few suggestions, see the recipes beginning on page 85.

OTHER TOLERABLE EDIBLES

There are some creatures living in our waters that look obnoxious and are repulsive to touch. When you get past all that, some are gourmet delicacies and others quite edible if one is hungry enough. I always wonder, who was the first starving person to tear into an artichoke and discover the delicious heart?

ABALONE

For the foreseeable future, the northern Abalone (*Haliotis Kamschatkana*) will have to yield to its cousins in California to satisfy the appetite for this delectable shellfish. Surveys have revealed a continuing decline in the number and size of northern abalone, leading to a complete ban on all harvest. In Washington State, I'm told, that ban will likely last into the year 2010.

Abalone (*Haliotis kamschatkana*)

OCTOPUS

Northwest waters are home to the largest octopus in size and number in the world. This shy and retiring creature has erroneously been made the villain in countless Hollywood movies. In real life, the last thing it wants to do is attack humans. This mollusk *(Octopus dofleini)* can measure up to twelve feet in diameter and can weigh 120 pounds.

Most of its edible meat comes from the arms, or tentacles, and has a clam-like flavor. It is usually "chewy-tough," requiring tenderizing as a large clam would.

Octopus *(Octopus dofleini)*

Octopus are usually found hiding in caves in rocky areas by scuba divers, but occasionally one will attach itself to a crab or shrimp trap for a quick trip to the surface when the trap is pulled. It is also not uncommon for one to attach to an anchor, for a ride to the surface while the boat gets underway.

It can become a ticklish situation when you get an octopus on deck. What do you do with it? It can move through any opening large enough for its hard beak to pass through. I once brought a small one aboard in a shrimp trap, from which it quickly escaped and took refuge under a boat seat. As we turned our attention to landing more shrimp traps, we didn't notice the 'pus sneaking up the back of the seat until it came "eye-to-eye" with my five-year-old son. With a yelp and within the blink of an eye, my son was perched upon the windshield. Then the really loud sounds began! To this day, my grown son HATES octopus!

Octopus must be caught with hands or instruments like shrimp traps which do not penetrate the octopus. When an octopus is caught with a hook and line, it can be kept.

SCALLOPS

Spiny Scallop, top row

Pink Scallop, bottom row

Pink or Spiny Scallops *(Chalmys)* are common in northern waters, but usually the only evidence is empty shells washed up on beaches. These unique, clam-like swimming bivalves jet through the water by quickly closing a valve and ejecting a stream of water through a small hole. Large schools of scallops entertain scuba divers by resembling a cloud of sets of dentures opening and closing, while moving erratically backward. They are harvested almost exclusively by commercial trawl nets in deep water, but can occasionally be found in shallows at low tide. Catching them can be a challenge, Got a butterfly net?

Rock Scallops *(Hinnites multirugosus)* present another challenge for sportsmen. Living below the low tide mark in rocky areas, rock scallops may be completely camouflaged with tube worms and barnacles. When found, they are extremely good eating. This is an unfamiliar shellfish because of the difficulty of harvesting it.

Rock Scallop, left, Weathervane Scallop, right. (WDFW)

Weathervane scallops (*Pecten caurinus*) are beautiful, tasty and also unfamiliar. They can grow to nine inches across, but are never found in less then 60 feet of water. Found on muddy or sandy bottoms at great depths, they are usually only taken as an incidental catch by commercial drag nets tilling the ocean bottom.

SEA CUCUMBER

Here's one that even hard-core mariners have a hard time dealing with. The sea cucumber *(Parastichopus Californicus)* is ugly, with a wart covered reddish skin, and slimy, squishy feel. When lifted out of the water, it will relieve itself with a stream of water that has been trapped inside, and deflate in a truly obscene fashion. It will then twitch and squirm when you slit it from end to end, like the huge worm it really is.

After it is laid open, five bands of muscle will be seen running lengthwise. Peel the muscle away from the skin and dice. The flavor is very rewarding, much

Sea Cucumber

like that of scallops, with the tender meat tasting good sauteed or in chowder.

Sea cucumber are commonly brought to the surface after being snagged from a reef on a bottomfishing hook, or after being found in the deeper tidal pools when one is wading on rocky beaches.

SEA URCHINS

The sea urchin really tests the hunger of beach combers and divers. These underwater pincushions come in three varieties: red urchin *(Strongylocentrotus)*, found in the San Juan Islands; green urchin *(S. drobachiensis)*, abundant in Puget Sound; and purple urchin *(S. purpuratus)*, common in tide pools and shallow water.

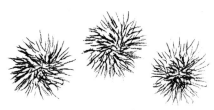

Sea Urchins

Many people cannot get past the sight and feel of these creatures, but they are one of Washington State's most widely exported sea food delicacies. Divers harvest multi-millions of pounds annually for export, mainly to Japanese markets.

Encased within the heavy shell, which is covered by hundreds of sharp spines, are five sections of tiny, yellowish-orange, egg-like roe, the edible portion. After cracking open the shell, this roe can be eaten raw with a spoon (the preferred method), or slightly cooked, breaded and spread upon crackers.

Shelf life, after being removed from the water, is measured in hours. Urchin dive boats are distinguished by the air compressors mounted on their decks which are connected to long air lines enabling divers to stay down for long periods. They can be seen delivering catches to docks in Friday Harbor, on San Juan Island. Waiting trucks drive the catch onto ferries and hurry to Sea-Tac Airport to meet waiting aircraft, which fly the harvest to Japan.

TOXINS

Clams, oysters, mussels and, to a lesser extent, crab all act as water filters, gathering in and retaining anything suspended in the water in which they live. They concentrate hazardous toxins within their systems. For that reason, it is important to ensure that the water from which you gather them is clean and free of both pollutants and toxins.

The most common toxin is referred to as "red tide." This condition occurs when air and water temperatures rise, while the winds and tides become calm. This causes an organism, *Gymnodinium breve*, to massively increase, to the extent that the water actually turns a reddish-brown. This is called a "bloom," and in itself it is not harmful to humans. However, as shellfish absorb water and filter it, they retain dangerous concentrations of this hazardous material. The rise in this algae-like organism does not have to be visible to become harmful, especially to elderly people.

Other toxins which do not discolor the water can become problems, also. There are 20 toxins responsible for paralytic shellfish poisoning known as "PSP." All are part of a group of molecular acids which are harmless until concentrated in shellfish. Amnesic shellfish poisoning, "ASP," is another toxin caused by an unusual amino acid, "domoic acid."

Ingestion of contaminated shellfish results in a wide variety of symptoms depending on the toxin present, it's concentration in the shellfish, and the amount of contaminated shellfish consumed. In the case of PSP, the effects are predominantly neurological and include tingling, burning, numbness, drowsiness, incoherent speech and respiratory paralysis.

Less severe are symptoms related to ASP poisoning, which may be observed as a general mild gastrointestinal disorder. Nausea, vomiting, diarrhea, and abdominal pain accompanied by chills, headache and fever can ruin a good dinner which was contaminated with ASP. Symptoms of these poisonings may occur anywhere from a few minutes to a couple of hours after eating.

All these toxins are rare in northwest waters, due to the cooler climate and colder water temperatures. To avoid them, call the local Red Tide Hotline, before gathering your shellfish.

Write your local Red Tide Hotline number in your tide guide.

California Department of Health Services
Shellfish Biotoxin information line: 800-553-4133.

Oregon Department of Fish and Wildlife
Shellfish Safety Hotline: 800-488-2474
Marine region information:
Newport (541) 867-4741
Charleston (541) 888-5515
Astoria (503) 325-2462.

Washington State Department of Health
Shellfish Biotoxin hotline: 800-562-5632.

B.C. Canada, Fisheries and Oceans
Safe Shellfish Harvest information 24-hour update:
(604) 666-2828.

Another important number for Washington residents:
The Shellfish Rule Change Hotline: 866-880-5431.

RECIPES: IT'S TIME TO EAT

The recipes here are all simple to prepare. They require a minimum of condiments. They can be used in a campsite over a fire or campstove, or aboard a boat equipped with simple cooking equipment. There are even a couple for the microwave, at home or aboard.

SERVING TIP: Pack hot, cooked Basmati or other white rice into a well buttered ring mold. Let it stand a few minutes to set up, then unmold onto a serving platter. Fill the hollow with shrimp/prawn tails, crab legs, fried clams or oysters, or any combination of seafood. Add your favorite vegetable for an attractive meal.

BEACH AND BARNYARD:

Just as fish and red meat make a popular "surf and turf" entree, shellfish and schnitzel are partners. Any of the following recipes can be served with a cut of pork. Bacon, chops or sausage will enhance the flavor of your favorite shellfish dinner.

An easy way to use all species of your days catch:

SEAFOOD SOUP

1/3 c. chopped green onion
2 sticks butter

2 pkg. half & half
1 large can cream
2 cans cream of mushroom soup
1 small can chopped mushrooms
1 heaping tsp. cayenne
Salt & pepper to taste
1/2 lb. boiled crayfish tails
1/2 lb. boiled crabmeat
1/2 lb. raw shrimp, peeled

Saute green onions in butter approximately 5 minutes.
Add remaining ingredients and simmer for 30 minutes.

Do not bring to a boil.

CALAMARI and SQUID RECIPES

A traditional way of cooking calamari is to bread it and pan or deep-fry it.

FRIED SQUID

Cleaned squid cut into 1-inch rings
Flour
Milk, or egg beaten with 1 tsp. water
2/3 c. bread crumbs mixed with 1/3 c. Parmesan Cheese
Oil, olive, peanut or vegetable per choice

Roll squid rings in flour, dip in milk (or egg mixture), roll in crumb mixture. Allow to sit a few minutes to stick the crumbs. Fry quickly in oil until golden brown. (about 1 minute on medium heat)

HOW ABOUT AN APPETIZER?

3 lbs. cleaned squid mantles

1/2 cup sour cream
1/2 cup mayonnaise
2 oz. chopped pimiento

1 tbsp. lemon juice
1 tsp. dried dill weed
Salt (try celery salt here) to taste

Cook mantles in boiling salted water 20 minutes or until tender.Drain. Chop squid into small pieces.
Mix squid, sour cream, mayonnaise, and pimiento.
Add lemon juice, dill weed and salt.
Serve chilled with crackers or chips.

My mom was a professional cook for 30 years. This is one of her favorite ways to prepare squid :

MOM'S CALAMARI SPAGHETTI SAUCE

    2 1/2 lbs. calamari

    5 tbsp. olive oil
    3 cloves garlic

    2 (28 oz.) cans plum tomatoes, crushed
    5 basil leaves
    1 tbsp. parsley, chopped
    Black pepper (to taste)
    Salt (to taste)

Wash, clean, slice calamari. Steam 5-10 minutes and save juice. Saute garlic in olive oil.
Add tomatoes, basil, parsley, pepper, salt. Simmer 30 minutes.
Add 1 cup of calamari juice. Simmer another 20 minutes.
Enough sauce for 1-1/2 pounds spaghetti. Enjoy!

MORE TRADITIONAL CALAMARI

    1-1/2 lb. calamari

    2 cloves garlic, pressed
    4 tbsp. butter

    4 tbsp. flour

    1/2 c. white wine
    1/2 c. water

    2 tbsp. thyme
    2 tbsp. parsley
    Pepper to taste

Clean calamari by removing tentacles and removing inksack and membrane. Slice body sack into circles and cut up tentacles.

Melt butter in large frying pan and brown garlic in butter. Add flour and mix thoroughly. Add wine and water to make sauce. Add spices.

Add calamari and cook until it turns opaque white. Grind fresh pepper into sauce. Serve over hot noodles. Sprinkle with Parmesan cheese.

Are you going to have a big party? Try this one :

CALAMARI AND SHELLFISH SAUCE

18 fresh cherry stone clams, scrubbed
3 lbs. mussels, scrubbed and beards removed
1 c. red wine

1/2 c. olive oil
1 onion, chopped
10 garlic cloves, minced

4 (28 oz.) cans ready-cut peeled tomatoes
1 tsp. oregano
3 tsp. fresh basil
3 tbsp. parsley
Pepper to taste
2 lbs. calamari (squid), cleaned and sliced
1 lb. large shrimp, cleaned and deveined
Red pepper flakes (optional)
2 lbs. linguine

In a large pot, steam clams and mussels in 1/2 cup red wine until they open. Discard any that don't open. Set aside and keep warm.

In a large Dutch oven, saute the onion and garlic in the olive oil (smells good). Add tomatoes, oregano, basil, parsley, remaining wine, pinch of salt, and pepper; simmer about 20 minutes.

Add the calamari, shrimp, mussels, and clams (with broth) and cook 5 minutes more or until shrimp are done.

Serve over linguine. Add crushed red pepper, if desired.
Serves: 8 to 10.

CALAMARI SALAD

          1-1/2 lbs. cleaned squid
          1/2 lemon
          1 c. diced celery
          1/2 c. red onion, sliced
          3 tbsp. lemon juice
          2 tbsp. drained capers
          2 tbsp. chopped parsley
          1 tbsp. olive oil
          1 clove garlic
          1/2 tsp. oregano
          Dash fresh ground pepper
          Lemon wedges for garnish

Cut cleaned squid into bite size pieces. Place in saucepan. Add lemon half and water to cover. Bring to a boil. Cook until tender, 5 minutes maximum. Drain and refrigerate until chilled.

To serve combine remaining ingredients except lemon wedges. Add squid and toss. Garnish with lemon wedges.

CALAMARI STEW

          1-1/2 lb. squid
          1/4 c. flour

          1/4 c. olive oil
          1/3 c. butter
          1 large onion, peeled & chopped

          2 cloves garlic, chopped
          12 parsley sprigs, leaves only

          1/2 c. chopped peeled tomatoes
          1/3 tsp. black pepper
          Pinch crushed red pepper
          Pinch of salt
          1/2 tsp. basil
          1/2 tsp. oregano

Clean squid and cut in 1 inch pieces. Sprinkle with flour.

Combine olive oil and butter in pan and heat.

Add onions and cook to medium brown. Add garlic and parsley; stir.
Add squid, stir, cover and cook for 20 minutes.

Add tomatoes, black and red pepper, salt, basil and oregano.
Stir, cover and cook for about 45 minutes.

Serve over a pasta of your choice.

Serves 4-5.

CALAMARI FROM AROUND THE WORLD: Italian-style

STUFFED CALAMARI

Whole squid mantles can be used in place of tube-shaped pastas.

>   2 lbs. cleaned mantles

>   3/4 cup ricotta cheese
>   3/4 cup grated mozzarella cheese
>   2 tbsp. chopped celery
>   1 tsp. dried oregano
>   1 tsp. dried basil
>   2 tbsp. grated Parmesan cheese

>   1/4 cup coarse bread crumbs
>   1 cup chopped mushrooms

>   2 cup marinara sauce
>   another 1/3 cup grated mozzarella cheese

Combine ricotta, 3/4 cup mozzarella, celery, oregano, basil,
Parmesan and mix well. Stir in bread crumbs and mushrooms. Stuff
mantles until plump but not packed. Close opening and secure with
a toothpick.

Pour small amount of marinara sauce into a 11 x 17 inch glass or
ceramic baking dish. Arrange squid in a single layer in dish.

Top with marinara sauce and bake uncovered at 350 degree for 20
minutes.

Top with remaining 1/3 cup mozzarella and bake another 10 minutes
or until squid is tender and filling is bubbly.

Serves four.

CALAMARI FROM AROUND THE WORLD : Greek

CALAMARI ATHENA

3 lbs. cleaned squid, whole or filets

2 tbsp. olive oil
1 cup chopped onion
1 clove garlic finely chopped

2-1/2 cups chopped tomatoes
1/2 cup chopped celery
1/2 tsp. salt
Dash of pepper
1/2 tsp. basil
1/2 tsp. oregano

Cook squid in boiling, salted water 20 minutes to an hour until tender. Drain. Cut into pieces.

Saute onion and garlic in hot oil until brown.
Add tomatoes, celery, seasonings and squid.

Cook until all ingredients are tender. Serve over rice.

Serves six.

CALAMARI FROM AROUND THE WORLD : Oriental

Use squid rings or pieces in your favorite stir-fry recipe.
They go well with Chinese or Japanese style vegetables cooked in a wok.

CLAM RECIPES

MOM'S FAMOUS CLAM FRITTERS

I first remember my mom telling the young people from the neighboring campsite at Westport, Washington, how to prepare the razor clams they had just dug. She recommended a quick and easy recipe for clam patties known as "fritters." Here it is:

1 cup pancake mix
1/4 tsp. salt
2 eggs (beaten)
3 tbsp. milk
1 "smidgen" (1 tbsp.) butter
2 cup "minced" clam

We carried a small portable hand grinder for "mincing;" finely chopped will suffice.

Blend all ingredients and form into patties in a saute skillet.
Brown both sides and serve buttered. (I like to drip a little honey on them.)

STEAMED CLAMS OR MUSSELS

Clams and mussels are usually steamed and served in the shell.

Allow them to "purge" themselves of sand and grit in clean water for a couple hours. Discard any with open shells.

Brush off any dirt and scrub "beards" from mussels, before placing in a large pan with an inch or two of water. I like to add a bit of garlic salt to the water. Cover and steam until shells open.

Discard any shells that did not open.

Serve hot with melted garlic butter.

Scoop meat out of shells with a fork and dip in butter.

"SMOKED" RAZOR (OR ANY OTHER) CLAMS

An easy way to prepare a great tasting snack that will keep, when refrigerated, 2 to 3 weeks:

> 15 razor clams cut in small pieces
> (or 40 to 50 "steamer" clam meats)
>
> 1/2 cup oil
> 3 tbsp. liquid smoke
> 2 tbsp. Worcestershire sauce
> 2 tbsp. lemon juice
> 1 tbsp. seasoning salt
> 1 tbsp. chili powder
> 1 tbsp. celery salt
> 1 tbsp. garlic powder

Combine oil and seasonings, then add clams.

Bake on a cookie sheet or shallow pan at 350" for an hour. Stir and drain frequently, saving the juices.

Store clams and juice in an airtight container.

DEEP FRIED CLAMS OR OYSTERS WITH POTATO

This recipe for frying clams or oysters will satisfy even picky eaters.

> 1/2 c. sour cream (milk will do)
> 1/4 c. flour
> 1/2 tsp. salt
> 1 egg, beaten
> 2 c. finely shredded potatoes
> 1 pint clam or oyster meats (drained and patted dry)
> Oil for deep frying

Stir together sour cream (or milk) and seasonings, and add to beaten eggs. Add potatoes and blend thoroughly. Add clams or oysters to mixture.

Heat oil to 375° in pan, wok or deep fryer. Drop mixture by large spoonfuls into hot oil. Keep morsels separated so they float freely, one layer deep. Fry until golden brown, about 2 to 3 minutes.

Remove and drain on paper towels.

CLAM CHOWDER CLAYTON

8 slices bacon

1 onion, chopped

2 or 3 large peeled potatoes

1/2 tsp. thyme
1/2 tsp. pepper
1 can mushroom soup
1 can cream of celery soup
1 can water
1 can (13 oz.) evaporated milk
2 cans minced clams, or 1 to 1-1/2 c. fresh ground clams

Cut bacon into 1/4 inch pieces and fry together with onion until tender and slightly crisp.

Cut potatoes into 1 inch cubes and place in pan with enough slightly salted water to cover potatoes. Boil until tender, but firm. Add drained bacon and onion. Stir in remaining ingredients and simmer on low heat.

Mix 3 tbsp. flour with enough water to make a thick paste (no lumps). Add to chowder. Cook until thickened. Add water if thinner chowder is desired. Add 1 c. parmesan cheese. Serve with French bread or rolls.

FRIED CLAMS OR OYSTERS

1 pint of steamed clam meats
or small uncooked, shucked oyster meats

1 c. flour
1 c. bread crumbs (optional)

2 eggs, beaten
Salt and pepper to taste
1/2 c. butter
lemon wedges

Drain clams or oysters and pat dry. Mix flour with bread crumbs.

Combine beaten eggs with salt & pepper. Roll meats in eggs, then flour. Fry in melted butter until browned on both sides. Serve with lemon wedges.

CRAB RECIPES

AVOCADO STUFFED WITH CRABMEAT

1/2 c. mayonnaise
1/2 c. stiffly whipped cream
1/3 c. chili sauce
1 tbsp. grated onion.

Combine ingredients.
Add crabmeat and pile into avocado halves.

BAKED TOMATOES WITH CRAB STUFFING

1/2 lb. cooked, cleaned crab, or 1 (7 1/2 oz.) can crab

6 medium tomatoes

1 tbsp. butter
1/4 c. chopped onion
1/2 c. chopped celery
1/4 c. chopped green pepper

1 1/2 c. coarse dry bread crumbs
1 tsp. salt
1/8 tsp. pepper
1/2 tsp. basil
Grated parmesan cheese

Drain and slice crab, reserving 6 pieces of leg for garnish.

Cut slice from stem end of each tomato. Scoop out pulp and reserve, discarding seeds. Turn tomato shells upside down to drain.

Melt butter in skillet. Add onion, celery and green pepper and saute until tender. Chop reserved tomato pulp and add to skillet. Cook for a few minutes.

Remove from heat and add bread crumbs, salt, pepper, basil and crab.

Sprinkle insides of tomato shells with salt. Fill with crab mixture. Sprinkle with grated parmesan cheese.

Bake at 375° for 20 to 25 minutes, or until tomatoes are tender. Garnish each tomato with a reserved leg piece during the last five minutes of baking.

CRAB LASAGNA

Another way to stretch your crab catch and create a dish that has brought great reviews from everyone who has tried it:

1/2 lb. lasagna noodles, cooked and set aside

2 cans cream of mushroom soup
1/3 cup milk
1 "packed" cup crab meat

8 oz. pkg. cream cheese, softened
2 cup small curd cottage cheese
1 egg
1 onion, finely chopped
1 tsp. garlic powder
1 tsp. salt
1/2 tsp. pepper

4 tomatoes, sliced
1-1/2 cups grated cheese of choice for topping

Combine soup, milk and crab in bowl.

In another bowl, combine cream cheese, cottage cheese, egg, onion and seasonings.

Place 1 layer cooked noodles in buttered 9 x 13 inch dish. Cover with half of the cheese mixture, then all of crab mixture.
Add another layer of noodles, then the remaining cheese mixture, and a final layer of noodles.

Bake in 325 degree oven for 15 minutes.

Top with sliced tomatoes and 1-1/2 cups grated cheese. Bake 40 minutes more.

Let stand 15 minutes before serving

CRAB NOODLE

A good way to stretch your crab catch and prepare a tasty simple meal is with an inexpensive package. I always keep one on board.

Prepare a box of noodles and cheese, such as Noodle-Roni, per package directions. During the last minute of cooking stir in a half pound or more of shucked crab meat.

Here's another of my all-time favorites. Have you detected yet that I'm pretty fond of cheeses and cilantro? And I don't have room to carry a prepared pie crust.

J.D.'s CRAB QUICHE (or "who needsa-da-crusta?")

1 cup fresh mushrooms, finely sliced
2 tbsp. butter

4 eggs
1 cup sour cream or IMO
1/2 pint small curd cottage cheese
1/2 cup grated Parmesan cheese
4 tbsp. flour
1 tsp. (heaping) onion powder
1/4 tsp. salt
Clipped cilantro leaves, to taste

2 cup (1/2 pound) shredded Monterey Jack cheese
1 "packed" cup crabmeat

In a medium skillet, sauté mushrooms in butter until tender. Remove with fork and drain on paper towels.

In a large bowl, blend well the eggs, sour cream, cottage cheese, Parmesan cheese, flour, onion powder, salt and cilantro.

Stir in mushrooms, cheese and crab meat.

Pour into a greased 10 inch baking dish and bake at 350° for about 45 minutes, until a toothpick or knife inserted near the center comes out dry. Quiche should be puffed and golden brown.

Let stand 5 minutes before cutting into wedges.

Ashore, you can substitute 1/2 pound of shredded ham for the crab, but it will not be as good.

Serves 8.

CRAYFISH RECIPES

Crayfish, Crawfish, or Crawdad, whatever you call them, they eat well. Here's the simplest method:

BOILED CRAYFISH

Select 24 good-size crayfish (live).

In a large pan, bring to a boil enough water to cover crayfish.

Dump the live crayfish into the scalding water (this is to stop offensive secretions from being forced through the crayfish).

Then take the crayfish out after three minutes, remove the tails and shell and veins. (Prepare like shrimp.)

CRAWFISH A-2 FAY (Étoufée)

Here's one of my favorites. Works with shrimp and crab meat as well.

> 2 lbs. peeled crawfish tails
> Salt, pepper, and cayenne pepper
>
> 1/4 lb. butter
> 1 c. chopped onions
> 1/2 c. chopped bell peppers
> 4 cloves garlic, minced
> 1/2 c. chopped celery
>
> 2 tbsp. crawfish fat
> 2 c. cold water
>
> Onion tops and parsley
> 2 tbsp. cornstarch

Season crawfish with salt and pepper. Set aside.

Melt butter in heavy pot; add onions, bell peppers, garlic, celery and cook, stirring constantly, until vegetables are wilted. When wilted, add crawfish fat and 1-1/2 cups water. Bring to a boil; cover; reduce heat and cook for 30 minutes, stirring occasionally.

Dissolve cornstarch (2 tablespoons for 2 pounds) in 1/2 cup of water. Add to crawfish mixture. Add onion tops and parsley and simmer another 10 minutes!

OK, lets go all out and get fancy:

CRAYFISH ELEGANTE

1 lb. crayfish tails slightly boiled, cooled and shelled

1/2 c. butter

1 bunch green onions, chopped
1 small onion, chopped
1/2 green pepper, chopped
1 clove garlic, minced
1/2 c. chopped parsley

3 tbsp. flour

1 pt. half & half

3-4 tbsp. dry sherry
Salt and pepper to taste

Vermicelli, cooked and warm

In half of butter, sauté crayfish for about 10 minutes.
Remove from pan.

In remaining butter, sauté all vegetables until tender. Cook on low
fire so vegetables won't become too brown.

Blend in flour. Stir well.

Gradually add cream, stirring until thickened.
Add sherry, salt and pepper.

Pour over cooked, warm vermicelli.
Toss well and serve.

CRAYFISH FETTUCCINI CASSEROLE

Maybe something a little more complicated to impress dinner
guests?

1-1/2 c. butter

3 onions, chopped
2 bell peppers, chopped
1 stalk celery, chopped
2 cloves garlic

1-2 lbs. shrimp or crayfish

1/4 c. flour

1 lb. Velveeta cheese, diced
1 pt. half & half
Salt, red and black pepper
2 tsp. jalapeno relish

Cooked noodles

Melt butter in pot; add onions, peppers, celery and garlic and cook to soften. Add seafood and cook 15 minutes.

Add 1/4 cup flour to thicken. Cook for 5 minutes, stirring often. Add Velveeta and everything else, cook for 15 more minutes.

Combine noodles and sauce. Pour into greased casserole dish and sprinkle with Parmesan cheese. Bake in oven 350° for 15 minutes.

Or just a good ol' down South staple:
CRAYFISH JAMBALAYA

2 sticks butter
1 large onion, chopped
1/4 c. green onions, chopped
1/3 c. green pepper, chopped
1/3 c. celery, chopped
2 cloves garlic, chopped
2 tbsp. parsley, chopped

2 cans cream of celery soup
2 tbsp. Worcestershire sauce
2 tbsp. Kitchen Bouquet

2 lb. crayfish

2 c. cooked rice

Sauté vegetables in butter; add soup, Worcestershire sauce and Kitchen Bouquet. Cook for 20 minutes over LOW HEAT.

Add crayfish and cook 30 minutes.
Add rice, serve hot.

MUSSELS ON THE HALF SHELL

Steamed, mussels (and large clams) can be served on a half shell.
Large Blue Mussels work best for this recipe.

> 1/2 cup green onion, finely chopped.
> 1/2 red pepper, finely chopped
> 1/2 medium yellow onion, finely chopped
> Juice from one lemon or 1 tbsp. concentrated lemon juice
> 2 tbsp. soy sauce
> 1 c. grated parmesan cheese
> 1/4 c. soft butter

Remove steamed meat from shells and set aside. Save the shells.

Blend all ingredients, except meat, well.

Place meat in half shells. Sprinkle mixture over meats. Broil until
lightly brown. This takes about 10 minutes, but watch carefully not
to burn them.

JACK MUSSELS

> 4 tbsp. butter
> 2 tbsp. flour
>
> 1 cup light cream
>
> 1 tsp. Worcestershire sauce
> 1/3 tsp. pepper
> 1 lb. mussel meats
>
> 1/2 cup grated Monterey Jack cheese

Cook 2 tbsp. butter and the flour over medium heat 2 minutes,
stirring constantly. Remove from heat and whip in the cream,
whisking until smooth. Stir in Worcestershire, pepper and mussels.

Pour the mixture into a 1-quart baking dish.

Top with the cheese and then the bread crumbs.
Melt the remaining butter and pour over the crumbs.

Bake 12 minutes at 375 degrees, then place under broiler just long
enough to lightly brown the top. Serves 2 or 4.

COZZE a la ARANCIONE   (Mussels a la Orange)*

    1 oz, butter
    1/2 tsp. shallots, chopped
    2 tbsp. leeks, sliced

    1/8 c. Tuaca
    1/4 c. fresh squeezed orange juice
    12 oz. bearded mussels

    1/2 c. heavy cream

    3 tbsp. peeled, seeded, and chopped tomato
    1/2 tsp. chopped parsley
    Salt
    White pepper

    1/4 tsp. orange zest

Saute shallots and leeks in butter over low heat until lightly wilted, about 2 minutes. Add Tuaca, orange juice and mussels. Cover and steam.

Remove mussels when opened, and keep warm.

Add cream to sauce; reduce over high heat by one-third.
Add tomatoes, parsley, salt, and white pepper to taste. Heat through.
Pour over mussels. Sprinkle with orange zest and fresh watercress.

Arrange mussels, open shell up. Do not completely cover with sauce.

* from Celebrate 100: The Washington State Centennial Cookbook (Romar Books Ltd./Evergreen Pacific Publishing Ltd). Recipe submitted to that 1989 centennial edition by the "il fiasco" restaurant of Bellingham, Washington.

MUSSEL SOUP

    1 tbsp garlic powder
    1/3 cup olive oil
    1 can Italian stewed tomatoes, cut in large pieces
    1/2 cup finely chopped peppers (red or yellow are attractive here)
    Lemon juice to taste
    1 pound mussel meat

Combine all ingredients and bring just to a boil. Serve with French bread and lemon slices. Serves 4.

OYSTER RECIPES

BARBECUED OYSTERS

A quick and easy way to cook oysters, and by far the easiest means to open them, is on the grill or in the oven.

Simply wash your oyster shells so you are not serving sand on your plates. Lay shells on your barbecue grate or oven grill, "bowl" side down, "flat" side up. Heat until shells open, pull top off and cover with your favorite barbecue sauce.

NOTE: This is also the way to serve OYSTERS ON THE HALF SHELL. Substitute butter for the barbecue sauce and add a dash of Tabasco sauce.

GUN CLUB OYSTER STEW

The oldest continuously operating gun club in Washington State is the North Whidbey Sportsmen's Association, in Oak Harbor. Longtime member, Harris Eloph, has been making the World's Best Oyster Stew for every January meeting for the past 20 years.

To feed 40 hungry sportsmen, Harris uses one gallon of large oysters cut into bite size portions. Put all the oysters and all the juice from the gallon container, along with a half pound of butter, in a large pot.

Heat to barely bubbling, but NOT BOILING. Turn down and simmer at least four hours—the longer the better. Harris says, "At a simmer you can't hurt it; but if you boil it, the oysters will become as tough as rubber."

That's it! No spices or other ingredients.

Serve with warm, but not hot enough to scald, whole milk and butter (one gallon of milk to 1/4 pound of butter). Use a ladle to scoop a portion of stew into a bowl, then scoop an equal portion of warm milk into the bowl. Salt and pepper it to taste, and serve with "oyster crackers" or saltines.

For smaller gatherings, a quart of oysters with a quart of milk and equivalent reductions of butter portions will suffice. Remember the "secret:" simmer the oysters in their own juice with butter for as long as possible on low heat. Stir occasionally.

OYSTERS FROM AROUND THE WORLD: Italian

OYSTER ITALIAN

> 1 dozen shucked oysters (save bottom halves)
> 3 cloves garlic, crushed and cooked in 3 tbsp. butter
>
> Salt and pepper to taste
>
> 1 cup bread crumbs
> 2 tbsp. chopped cilantro
> 1/2 tbsp. oregano
> 2 tbsp. olive oil

Rub the shell halves with the garlic butter and place the oysters back in them. Add salt and pepper. Mix bread crumbs, cilantro, and oregano with oil, and sprinkle over oysters. Place shells on a baking tray and broil for about 10 minutes. Serve on the half shells.

OYSTERS FROM AROUND THE WORLD: Chinese

CHINESE BRAISED OYSTERS

> 1 qt. shucked oysters
>
> 1/4 cup olive oil
> Chopped garlic, ginger, and green onions to taste
> Salt
>
> 1/4 cup oyster sauce
> 1 tbsp. sugar
> Pepper
> 1 tbsp. soy sauce
>
> 1 tsp. corn starch

Boil 2 cups of water and pour over oysters in a large bowl, set aside 15 minutes, then drain, retaining 1/4 cup of the water.

Meanwhile, heat oil in wok and simmer garlic, ginger, onions and salt 5 minutes. Mix oyster sauce, sugar and pepper together, then mix all ingredients in wok, quickly thickening with cornstarch and the retained water.

OYSTER STUFFING

Many people swear by an oyster stuffing for holiday birds, from turkey or geese to chicken and ducks. Here's an easy one to prepare.

8 oz. shucked small oysters, chopped and drained (reserve liquid)
2 cup garlic & herb stuffing mix
2 cup cornbread stuffing mix
1/2 cup chopped celery
1/2 cup chopped onion
3/4 cup chicken broth

Combine oysters with stuffing mixes, celery and onion, then stir in oyster liquid and chicken broth. Place in an ungreased 2 quart baking dish. Bake 30 minutes at 350 degrees. This will be enough to stuff 8 pounds of poultry. Double recipe to stuff up to 16 pounds.

SCALLOP RECIPES

BROILED SCALLOPS

Place lightly buttered scallops on a flat baking sheet and sprinkle with salt and pepper. Broil 5 to 6 minutes or until lightly browned. Serve with lemon juice.

SCALLOPS SAUTE

1-1/2 lbs. bay scallops
Flour
6 tbsp. olive oil
1/3 c. chopped cilantro
2 finely chopped garlic cloves
1 tbsp. chives
Salt and pepper to taste

Thoroughly clean scallops and roll them in flour. Place in heated olive oil and cook rapidly while tossing lightly. As the scallops are cooking, add the chopped garlic and chives and mix well. Add cilantro and toss with the scallops. Serve with lemon wedges. Variation: omit garlic and add 1 tsp. tarragon, 1 tsp. chives and parsley.

SCALLOPS & MUSHROOMS IN CREAMY GARLIC SAUCE OVER LINGUINE

OK, lets whip out something that *sounds* really fancy to impress the neighbors when they come for dinner. Little will they know how easy it was to prepare. This will work equally with shrimp or prawns.

> 3/4 pound bay scallop or sea scallops, cut 4 ways.
> 1 cup sliced fresh mushrooms
> 2 tbsp. butter, plus 1 more
>
> 1 tbsp. flour
> 1/2 tsp. salt
> 1/4 tsp. pepper
>
> 1/3 cup cream or milk
>
> 1/3 cup chopped green onion
> 1 or 2 cloves minced garlic
> 2 tbsp. chopped cilantro
>
> 1 (1 lb.) package linguine, cooked
> Grated Parmesan cheese

Saute scallops and mushrooms in 2 tbsp. butter until almost done. Set aside.

Melt other tbsp. butter in skillet; be careful not to brown it. Add flour, salt, and pepper, stirring slowly for 2-3 minutes for flour to blend. Add cream or milk slowly to make a smooth sauce.

Stir in scallops, mushrooms, green onion, garlic and cilantro. Serve over cooked linguine and top with Parmesan cheese.

PAN FRIED SCALLOPS

Here's my favorite. It appears elegant when served but is easy to prepare and always produces raves from first time dinner guests:

> 1-1/2 lbs. rinsed bay scallops
> 1/3 cup dry bread crumbs
>
> 1/2 cup butter, plus another 1/2 cup set aside
> 1/4 tsp. salt
> 1/4 tsp. lemon pepper (optional)
>
> 1/3 cup lemon juice
> 1 tbsp. finely chopped cilantro
> 2 cup cooked rice (basmati is best)

Roll scallops in bread crumbs.
Gently melt butter in frying pan. Do not brown. Mix in salt and lemon pepper then gently add scallops; fry slowly over low heat, turning often until golden brown, about 10 minutes.

Remove scallops and gently arrange upon awaiting beds of rice.

Add remaining butter, lemon juice and cilantro to frying pan and melt together; pour over scallops and serve 4 people.

SHRIMP & PRAWN RECIPES

DEEP FRIED SHRIMP

> 40 shelled shrimp or 18 prawns
> 3 cups pancake mix
> 4 eggs
> 1-1/2 tbsp. salt
> 6 tbsp. melted butter
> 12 oz. flat beer
> Oil enough for deep frying

From the night before, save a can of opened beer so it can go flat (a moment of silence here).

The next morning, combine the pancake mix, eggs, salt and butter. Add the beer and refrigerate. Come dinner time, heat the oil to 350°. Dip the shelled shrimp/prawns in the batter and deep-fry for about a minute. Watch the batter turn brown.

SHRIMP COCKTAIL

3/4 c. chili sauce
1/4 c. lemon juice
1 tbsp. horseradish
1 tsp. minced onion
2 tsp. Worcestershire sauce
4 drops Tabasco sauce
Dash of salt
Shrimp (cooked and cleaned)

Combine ingredients except shrimp. Chill thoroughly. Spoon sauce into individual cocktail cups over chilled shrimp. Garnish cup by hooking several shrimp over rim of glass. Makes 1 cup of sauce.

SWEET AND SOUR SHRIMP

1/4 c. salad oil
1 c. green pepper, diced
1 c. celery, diced
1 c. onion, diced
2 tsp. flour
1-1/2 c. tomato juice
1/3 c. brown sugar
1/2 tsp. salt
1/4 c. lemon juice
1 tbsp. grated lemon rind

1-1/2 lb. fresh cooked shrimp
1 small can sliced pineapple

Saute pepper, celery and onion in oil. Do not brown.
Add flour and blend.

Add tomato juice, sugar, salt, lemon juice and rind. Cook 5 minutes.

Add shrimp and pineapple slices. Heat and serve with rice.
Serves 6.

J.D.'s fetish with cheeses continues here, this time with "Feta".

PRAWN LA-FETA

1 cube butter
2 tbsp. garlic powder
12-18 prawns, shelled, deveined and butterflied
1/4 cup white wine
Juice of lemon to taste
3 good size green onions, chopped
Finely clipped cilantro to taste
1 large tomato, diced
Small can sliced black olives
3/4 cup crumbled feta cheese
1/8 tsp. pepper

Melt butter in a large skillet over medium heat. Add garlic and prawns, constantly stirring and turning, about 30 seconds. Add wine, lemon juice, green onions, cilantro, tomato and olives, continuing to stir until prawn turn light pink and are lightly firm. Remove from heat. Lightly cover with feta cheese and serve immediately.

Fresh bread served on the side is good for dipping in the delicious sauce.

CIOPPINO - SEAFOOD GUMBO

1/4 c. butter (or margarine)
2 medium onions, chopped
2 garlic cloves, pressed or minced
1/3 c. chopped parsley

1 bay leaf
2 c. dry white wine
1/2 tsp. thyme leaves
1/2 tsp. rosemary leaves
2 (14 oz.) cans chicken broth
1 c. water

1-1/2 lb. clams in the shell
1 1/2 lb. cod or red snapper
2 lb. crab in the shell

6 oz. large shell macaroni

3/4 lb. shrimp in shell
2 or 3 tomatoes, chopped

Melt butter in 6 quart kettle. Add onion, garlic and parsley. Cook until onion is soft, stirring often. Add bay leaf, wine, thyme, rosemary, broth and water. Simmer 15 minutes.

Rinse off clam shells, cut fish into 1 inch pieces, break legs off body of crab which is cleaned, but still in the shell.

Place crab legs and body, clams, noodles and fish into the kettle. Cover and simmer until noodles are done (10 minutes).

Add cleaned shrimp the last 3 minutes. Add tomatoes. Mix well. Serve while hot with French bread and your favorite wine.

IN CONCLUSION

Whether you are new to the Northwest marine scene or a longtime resident, adding shellfish to your culinary experience will greatly enrich your life. Tasty nutritious dinners gathered from nearby waters can make you healthier and happier.

Any meal or snack can be enhanced by including shellfish. Most folks can eat 1/3 pound of crab meat, 15 to 20 steamer clams, a dozen small oysters in shell or one pint shucked, or one pound of shrimp meat per sitting.

When preparing shellfish, remember not to overcook shellfish or any other seafood. It will become dry and tough if you do. Keep your cooking method and recipe simple, using a minimum of seasonings to allow the natural flavor of the shellfish to come through. When making chowder, use an amount of shellfish meat equal to the quantity of potatoes.

When gathering shellfish, only take the amount you can use for dinner. It is always best fresh, and never as good after being frozen or even refrigerated overnight. It's better to draw out the experience of gathering shellfish to another day, and again enjoy the fresh flavor.

Make your shellfish hunting a family adventure, and enjoy your healthy meal together.

APPENDIX A
Puget Sound Shellfish Site Maps*

How to Use the Maps and Indexes

The maps in this appendix identify many of the public shellfish sites around Puget Sound that offer some form of recreational opportunity, generally open to the public. These maps are meant for REFERENCE ONLY! The opening and closing of marine areas for shellfish gathering is constantly changing. State departments of health and departments of fish and wildlife cannot keep up with the changes on maps. So ALWAYS contact your local agencies before approaching any beaches. Some smaller beaches were difficult to show on maps of this scale and therefore were not included. Beaches with known boundary line or ownership problems are not listed. Maps 1-9 are two-page spreads. The northern section of each of the those maps is on the even numbered page. and the southern section on the opposite odd numbered page.

These charts are offered only as a reference to where different shellfish species are normally found. They should not be considred showing where they can be accessed due to private properties, closed beaches, or water quality problems.

Finding a Beach

The following section of this booklet contains two indexes and 10 maps. Every beach shown has a number next to it. However, only beaches with names are listed in the indexes. An alphabetical index by beach name is found preceding the maps, and a numerical index by beach number is found after the maps.

Requesting Information

Please refer to beaches by number and name when requesting information about a beach. It you know of any beach name corrections or new beaches to be added, please contact the Washington Department of Fish and Wildlife's Point Whitney Shellfish Laboratory at 360-796-4601.

Understanding Marine Biotoxin Closure Areas

The maps contain common landmarks used to describe closure areas on the marine biotoxin hotline. Referring to maps in this appendix will help you identify closure areas. See important toxin hotline numbers on page 83.

*Reprinted from Public Shellfish Sites of Puget Sound, a booklet originally prepared by the Washington Department of Fisheries in 1989 and revised in 1999 through the combined efforts of Washington departments of Health, Fish & Wildlife, Natural Resources, & Ecology; the Parks & Recreation Commission: the Puget Sound Water Quality Action Team. the Bremerton-Kitsap Co. Health District: the N. W. Indian Tribes. and the university of Washington Sea Grant Program. Maps created by Derry Suther and Randy Butler

Color Codes of the Maps

The environmental health of certain areas are color coded green, blue, yellow, and red on the maps. These areas have been adapted from commercial growing area classifications and give a generalized representation of the health of an area. Not all beaches within a colored area have been classified. These area health classifications are for bivalve shellfish only and are not intended for other types of shellfish harvested from the beach, such as crab.

Green color indicates areas that are generally approved for commercial and recreational shellfish harvest. However, a beach within green area that is unclassified (without a symbol by the beach) by the Washington Department of Health has not had a site specific evaluation. Harvesters should inquire with their local health department.

Blue color indicates areas that are conditionally open for commercial and recreational harvest. This means that under certain conditions, usually excessive rainfall, or seasonal boat useage, these areas have the potential to become contaminated. Harvesters should inquire with their local health department prior to harvesting on all beaches with this classification.

Yellow color indicates areas where harvesting is not advised due to the proximity to urban areas. Beaches in these areas are exposed to a number of sources with the potential for contamination from chemical and bacterial contaminants.

Red color indicates areas that are closed for commercial and recreational harvest. These areas have known contamination sources such as failing onsite sewage systems, agricultural runoff, marinas, and sewage treatment plant outfalls.

Unclassified areas of the maps without color have not been evaluated by the Washington Department of Health.

Because of changing conditions the accuracy of the maps cannot be guaranteed. Contact the local health department prior to harvesting on ANY beach.

Beach Index Abbreviations

CP - County Park HBR - Harbor
HD - Head
IS - Island
LT - Little
NWR - National Wildlife Refuge
PK - Park
PT - Point
REC - Recreation
RES - Reserve -
RKS - Rocks
USFS - United States Forest Service

Beach Index — Alphabetical

Beach Index — Alphabetical

Beach Index — Alphabetical

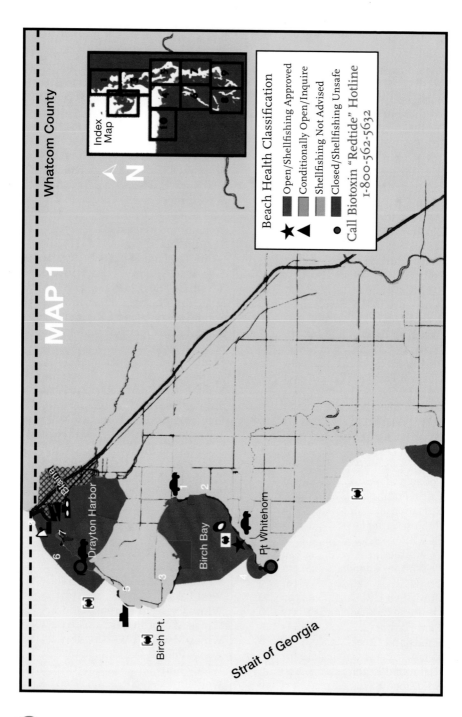

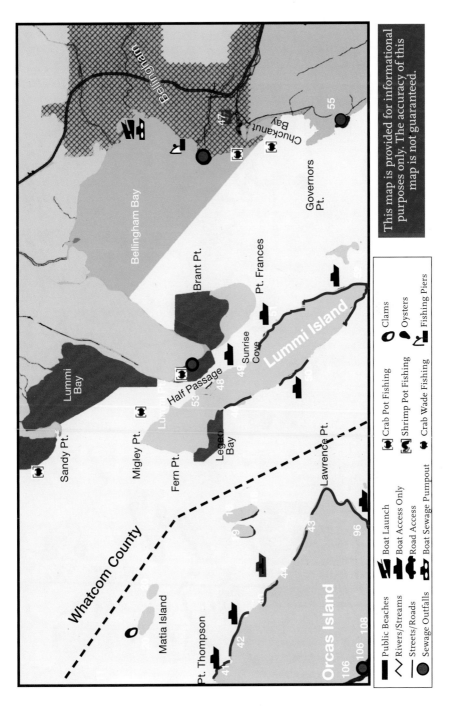

This map is provided for informational purposes only. The accuracy of this map is not guaranteed.

Legend:

Public Beaches
Rivers/Streams
Streets/Roads
Sewage Outfalls

Boat Launch
Boat Access Only
Road Access
Boat Sewage Pumpout

Crab Pot Fishing
Shrimp Pot Fishing
Crab Wade Fishing

Clams
Oysters
Fishing Piers

Map labels:

Bellingham
Chuckanut Bay
Governors Pt.
Bellingham Bay
Brant Pt.
Pt. Frances
Lummi Island
Sunrise Cove
Half Passage
Lummi Bay
Sandy Pt.
Migley Pt.
Fern Pt.
Legoe Bay
Lawrence Pt.
Whatcom County
Matia Island
Pt. Thompson
Orcas Island

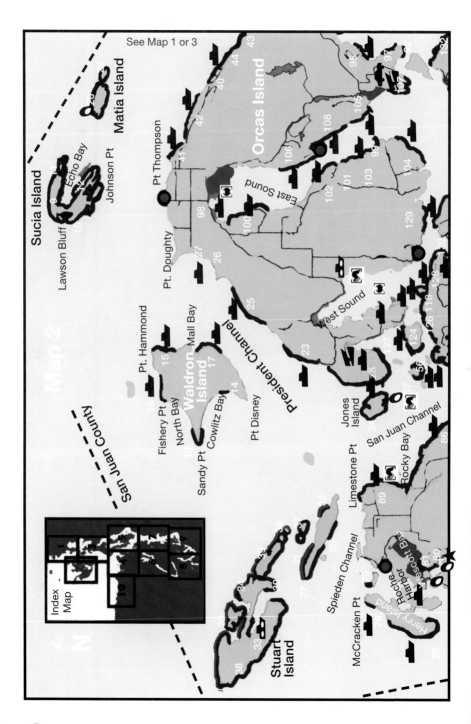

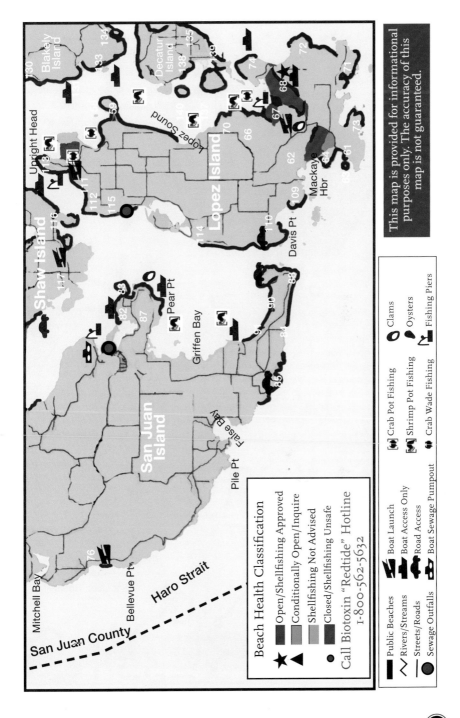

Beach Health Classification

- Open/Shellfishing Approved
- Conditionally Open/Inquire
- Shellfishing Not Advised
- Closed/Shellfishing Unsafe

★ ◄ ●

Call Biotoxin "Redtide" Hotline
1-800-562-5632

Public Beaches
Rivers/Streams
Streets/Roads
Sewage Outfalls

Boat Launch
Boat Access Only
Road Access
Boat Sewage Pumpout

Crab Pot Fishing
Shrimp Pot Fishing
Crab Wade Fishing

Clams
Oysters
Fishing Piers

This map is provided for informational purposes only. The accuracy of this map is not guaranteed.

Blakely Island
Decatur Island
Upright Head
Lopez Sound
Lopez Island
Mackaye Hbr
Davis Pt
Shaw Island
Pear Pt
Griffen Bay
San Juan Island
False Bay
Pile Pt
Mitchell Bay
Bellevue Pt
Haro Strait
San Juan County

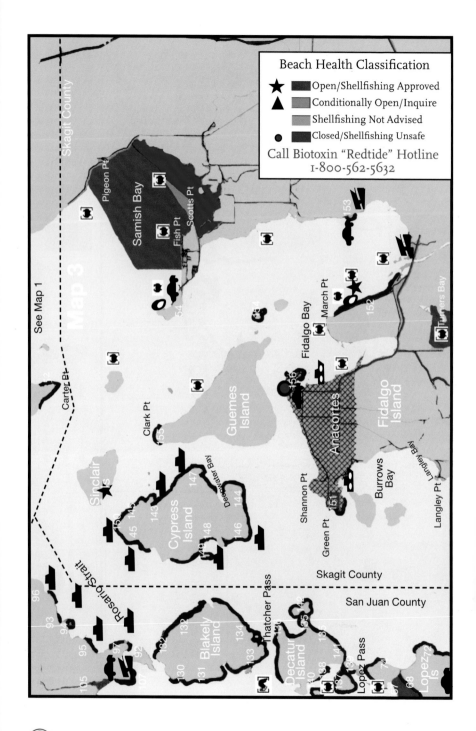

Beach Health Classification

★ Open/Shellfishing Approved
▲ Conditionally Open/Inquire
Shellfishing Not Advised
● Closed/Shellfishing Unsafe

Call Biotoxin "Redtide" Hotline
1-800-562-5632

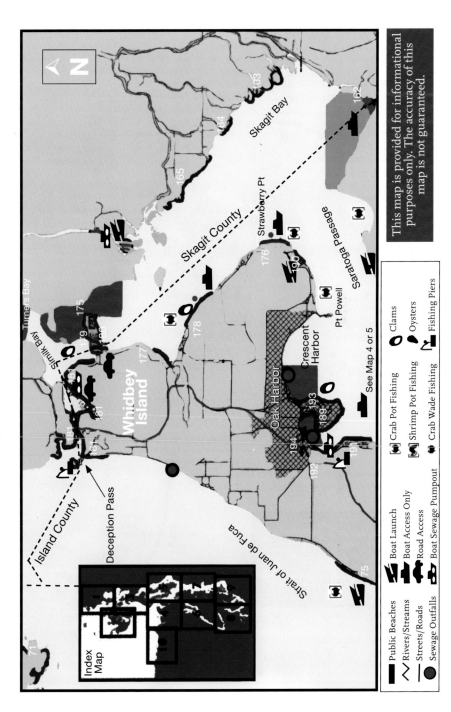

This map is provided for informational purposes only. The accuracy of this map is not guaranteed.

Legend:

- Public Beaches
- Rivers/Streams
- Streets/Roads
- Sewage Outfalls
- Boat Launch
- Boat Access Only
- Road Access
- Boat Sewage Pumpout
- Crab Pot Fishing
- Shrimp Pot Fishing
- Crab Wade Fishing
- Clams
- Oysters
- Fishing Piers

Skagit Bay
Skagit County
Strawberry Pt
Saratoga Passage
Pt Powell
Turner's Bay
Similk Bay
Whidbey Island
Crescent Harbor
Oak Harbor
See Map 4 or 5
Island County
Deception Pass
Strait of Juan de Fuca
Index Map

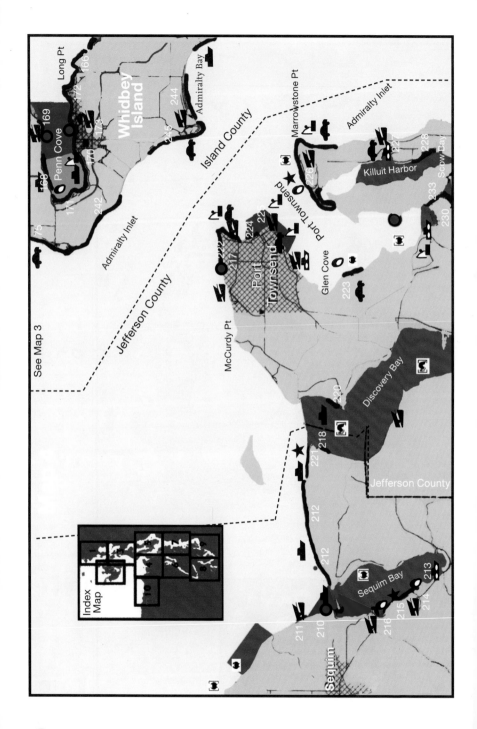

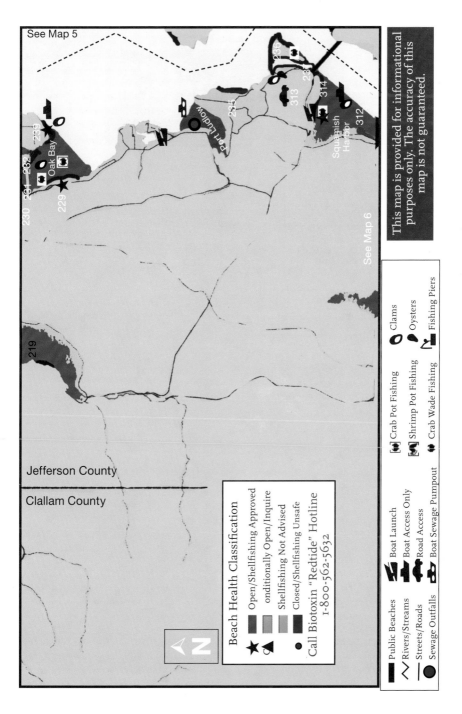

See Map 5

See Map 6

Port Ludlow

Oak Bay

Squamish Harbor

Jefferson County

Clallam County

This map is provided for informational purposes only. The accuracy of this map is not guaranteed.

Beach Health Classification

Open/Shellfishing Approved

Conditionally Open/Inquire

Shellfishing Not Advised

Closed/Shellfishing Unsafe

Call Biotoxin "Redtide" Hotline
1-800-562-5632

★ Public Beaches
◄ Rivers/Streams
— Streets/Roads
● Sewage Outfalls

Boat Launch
Boat Access Only
Road Access
Boat Sewage Pumpout

Crab Pot Fishing
Shrimp Pot Fishing
Crab Wade Fishing

Clams
Oysters
Fishing Piers

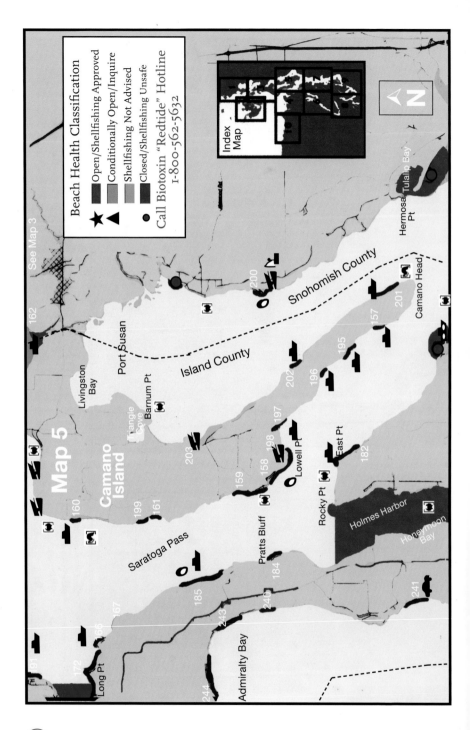

Map 5

Beach Health Classification

★ Open/Shellfishing Approved
◄ Conditionally Open/Inquire
  Shellfishing Not Advised
● Closed/Shellfishing Unsafe

Call Biotoxin "Redtide" Hotline
1-800-562-5632

Index Map

N

See Map 3

162

200

201

Snohomish County
Island County
Port Susan

157

195

196

202

197
198
158
159

203

160
199
161

Livingston Bay

Triangle Cove

Barnum Pt

Lowell Pt
East Pt

182

Rocky Pt

Holmes Harbor

Honeymoon Bay

Camano Island

Camano Head

Hermosa Tulalip Bay Pt

Saratoga Pass

Pratts Bluff

184

185

240

243

244

241

167

165

191

172

Long Pt

Admiralty Bay

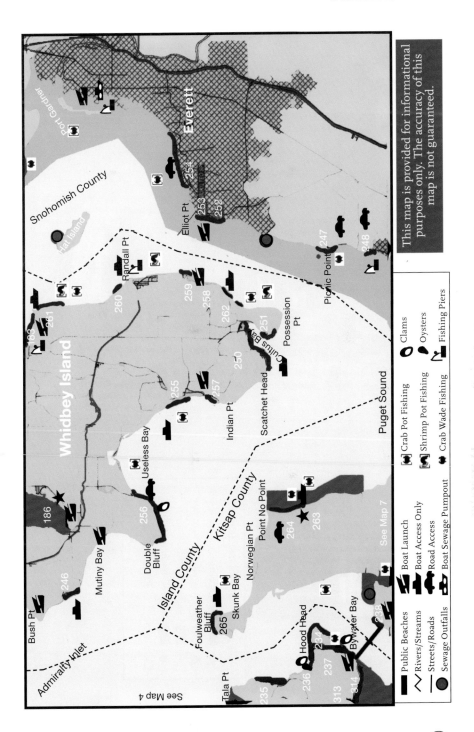

This map is provided for informational purposes only. The accuracy of this map is not guaranteed.

Everett

Snohomish County

Hat Island

Port Gardner

Elliot Pt

254
253
252

Picnic Point

247

248

Randall Pt

260

259
258
262

Possession Pt

251

Cultus Bay

230

189
261

Whidbey Island

255
257

Indian Pt

Scatchet Head

Puget Sound

Useless Bay

186

256

Double Bluff

Point No Point

264

263

See Map 7

Kitsap County

Norwegian Pt

Island County

246

Mutiny Bay

Foulweather Bluff

Skunk Bay

265

Bush Pt

Admiralty Inlet

See Map 4

Tala Pt

235

236

Hood Head

234

237

Bywater Bay

313
314

Public Beaches

Rivers/Streams

Streets/Roads

Sewage Outfalls

Boat Launch

Boat Access Only

Road Access

Boat Sewage Pumpout

Crab Pot Fishing

Shrimp Pot Fishing

Crab Wade Fishing

Clams

Oysters

Fishing Piers

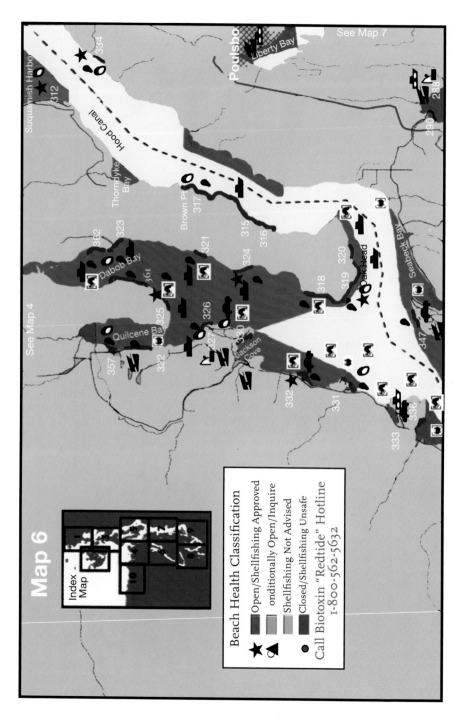

Map 6

Index Map

Beach Health Classification

★ Open/Shellfishing Approved

◄ Conditionally Open/Inquire

Shellfishing Not Advised

● Closed/Shellfishing Unsafe

Call Biotoxin "Redtide" Hotline
1-800-562-5632

See Map 7

See Map 4

Poulsbo

Liberty Bay

Suquamish Harbo

Hood Canal

Thorndyke Bay

Brown Pt

Dabob Bay

Quilcene Bay

Jackson Cove

Oak Head

Seabeck Bay

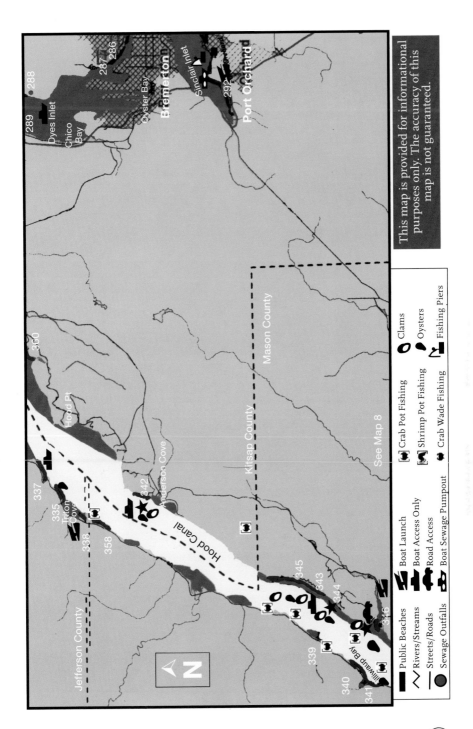

This map is provided for informational purposes only. The accuracy of this map is not guaranteed.

Clams
Oysters
Fishing Piers

Crab Pot Fishing
Shrimp Pot Fishing
Crab Wade Fishing

Public Beaches
Rivers/Streams
Streets/Roads
Sewage Outfalls

Boat Launch
Boat Access Only
Road Access
Boat Sewage Pumpout

See Map 8

Mason County
Kilsap County
Jefferson County

Hood Canal
Hood Pt
Anderson Cove
Triton Cove
Dosewallips

Dyes Inlet
Chico Bay
Oyster Bay
Bremerton
Sinclair Inlet
Port Orchard

Dewatto Bay
Lilliwaup Bay

288
289
287
286
292
360
337
335
338
358
342
345
343
344
346
339
340
341

127

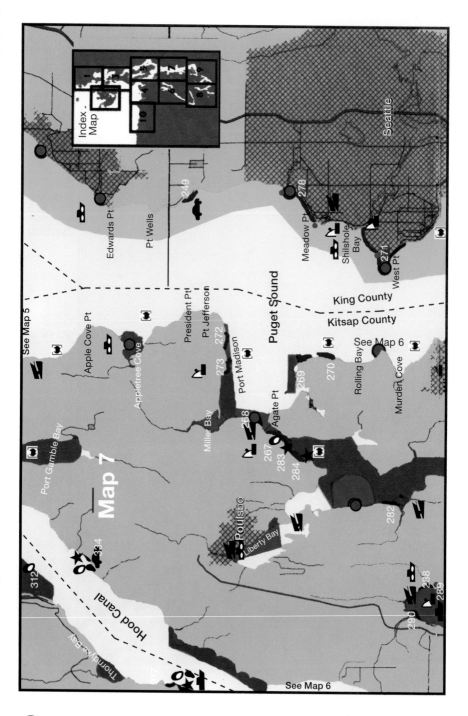

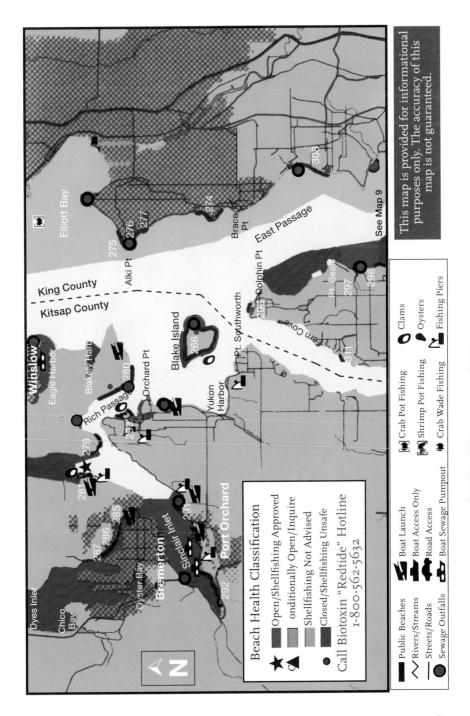

This map is provided for informational purposes only. The accuracy of this map is not guaranteed.

Beach Health Classification

- ★ Open/Shellfishing Approved
- Conditionally Open/Inquire
- Shellfishing Not Advised
- Closed/Shellfishing Unsafe

Call Biotoxin "Redtide" Hotline
1-800-562-5632

- ★ Boat Launch
- Boat Access Only
- Road Access
- Boat Sewage Pumpout

- Public Beaches
- Rivers/Streams
- Streets/Roads
- Sewage Outfalls

- Crab Pot Fishing
- Shrimp Pot Fishing
- Crab Wade Fishing

- Clams
- Oysters
- Fishing Piers

Elliott Bay
Winslow
Eagle Harbor
Blakely Harbor
Rich Passage
Orchard Pt
Blake Island
Yukon Harbor
Pt. Southworth
Dolphin Pt
Fern Cove
Pt. Beals
East Passage
Brace Pt
Alki Pt
King County
Kitsap County
Bremerton
Port Orchard
Sinclair Inlet
Oyster Bay
Chico Bay
Dyes Inlet

See Map 9

275
276
277
274
308
296
297
298
311
266
280
279
28
285
286
287
291
292

129

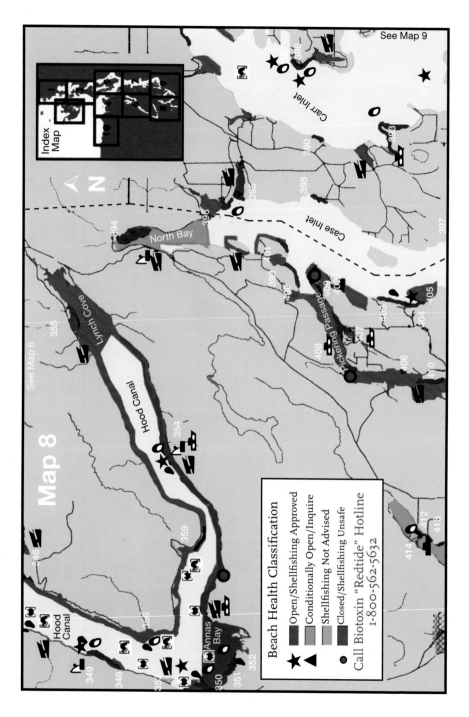

See Map 9

Carr Inlet

Case Inlet

Index Map

N

North Bay

Map 8

See Map 6

Lynch Cove

Hood Canal

Pickering Passage

Hood Canal

Annas Bay

Beach Health Classification

★ Open/Shellfishing Approved

◀ Conditionally Open/Inquire

Shellfishing Not Advised

● Closed/Shellfishing Unsafe

Call Biotoxin "Redtide" Hotline
1-800-562-5632

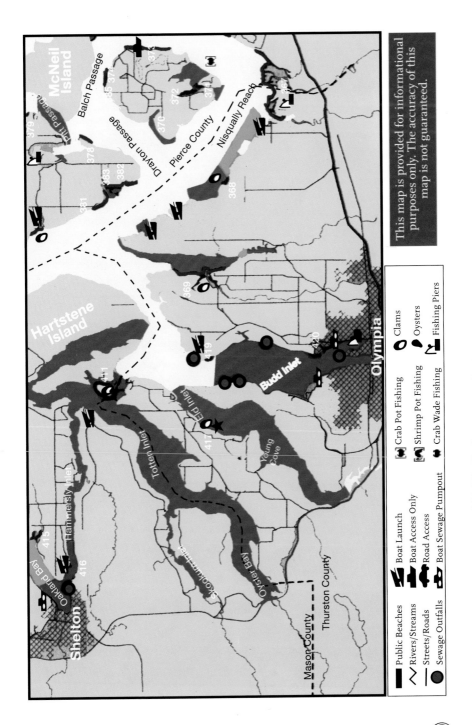

This map is provided for informational purposes only. The accuracy of this map is not guaranteed.

Clams
Oysters
Fishing Piers

Crab Pot Fishing
Shrimp Pot Fishing
Crab Wade Fishing

Boat Launch
Boat Access Only
Road Access
Boat Sewage Pumpout

Public Beaches
Rivers/Streams
Streets/Roads
Sewage Outfalls

McNeil Island
Balch Passage
Pitt Passage
Drayton Passage
Pierce County
Nisqually Reach
Hartstene Island
Olympia
Budd Inlet
Eld Inlet
Young Cove
Totten Inlet
Hammersley Inlet
Skookum Inlet
Oyster Bay
Oakland Bay
Shelton
Mason County
Thurston County

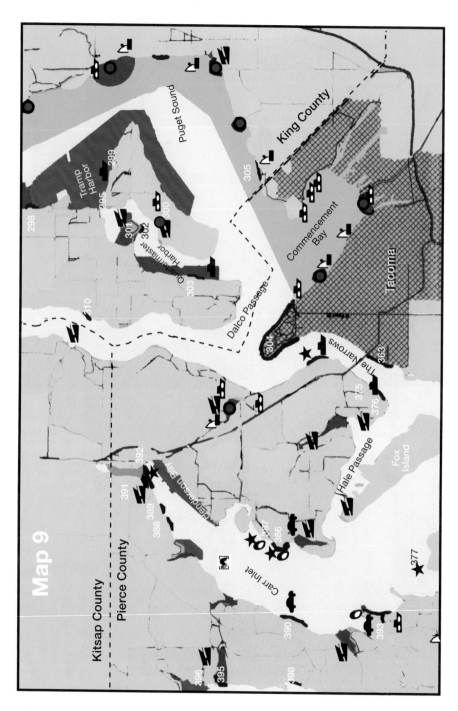

Map 9

Kitsap County

Pierce County

Puget Sound

Tramp Harbor

299

295

298

Quartermaster Harbor

300

301

302

303

305

King County

Commencement Bay

Tacoma

304

Dalco Passage

310

The Narrows

363

375

376

Hale Passage

Fox Island

377

392

391

389

388

Henderson Bay

Carr Inlet

387

386

390

393

396

395

398

Beach Health Classification

Open/Shellfishing Approved
Conditionally Open/Inquire
Shellfishing Not Advised
Closed/Shellfishing Unsafe

★
◀
●

Call Biotoxin "Redtide" Hotline
1-800-562-5632

This map is provided for informational purposes only. The accuracy of this map is not guaranteed.

Index Map

Public Beaches
Rivers/Streams
Streets/Roads
Sewage Outfalls

Boat Launch
Boat Access Only
Road Access
Boat Sewage Pumpout

Crab Pot Fishing
Shrimp Pot Fishing
Crab Wade Fishing

Clams
Oysters
Fishing Piers

Pitt Passage
McNeil Island
Balch Passage
Drayton Passage
Anderson Island
Nisqually Reach
Thurston County

378
383
382
381
368
367
371
372
370
373
374
385
364
365
366

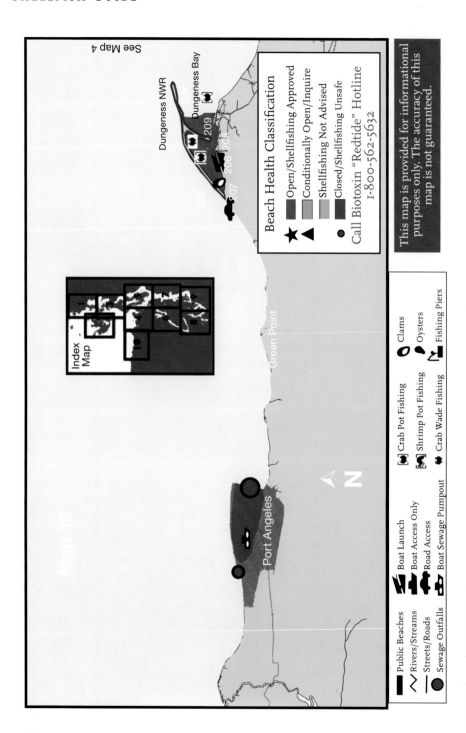

Map 10

See Map 4

Dungeness NWR

Dungeness Bay

209

208

207 206

205

Index Map

Green Point

Port Angeles

N

Beach Health Classification

- Open/Shellfishing Approved
- Conditionally Open/Inquire
- Shellfishing Not Advised
- Closed/Shellfishing Unsafe

★ ◀ ●

Call Biotoxin "Redtide" Hotline
1-800-562-5632

This map is provided for informational purposes only. The accuracy of this map is not guaranteed.

- Public Beaches
- Rivers/Streams
- Streets/Roads
- Sewage Outfalls

- Boat Launch
- Boat Access Only
- Road Access
- Boat Sewage Pumpout

- Crab Pot Fishing
- Shrimp Pot Fishing
- Crab Wade Fishing

- Clams
- Oysters
- Fishing Piers

Beach Index — Numerical

Beach Index — Numerical

Beach Index — Numerical

APPENDIX B
Oregon Coast Beaches–Northern Half

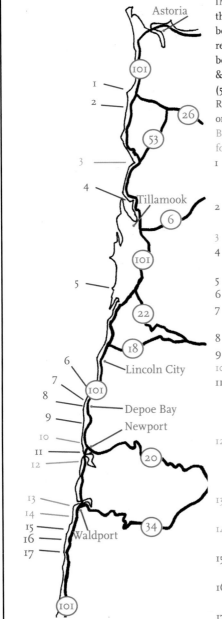

IMPORTANT NOTICE: The information on this chart is current as of the edition of this book. For the latest information on shellfish regulations and recommendations for Oregon beaches contact the Oregon Department of Fish & Wildlife: Newport (541.867.4741), Charleston (541.888.5515), or Astoria (503.325.2462).

RED TITLES: Shellfishing Restrictions imposed on this beach or area.

BLUE TITLES: Recommended as a beach or area for specific kinds of shellfishing.

1   Tillamook Head Beaches north of Tillamook Head are closed to razor clams July 15 - September 30.
2   Haystack Rock (Cannon Beach) Closed to clams and mussels.
3   Nehalem Bay Recommended for crabbing.
4   Netarts Bay Closed to clamming in posted shellfish preserves.
5   Cape Kiwanda Closed to clams and mussels.
6   Boiler Bay Closed to oysters.
7   Pirate Cove Closed to shellfishing in subtidal zone (below low-water mark).
8   Whale Cove Closed to shellfishing.
9   Otter Rock Closed to clams and mussels.
10 Agate Beach Recommended for clamming.
11 Yaquina Head/Yaquina Bay Yaquina Head closed to clams and mussels. Yaquina Bay closed to clamming in posted shellfish preserves.
12 South Beach State Park/South Jetty (South Beach) South Beach State Park recommended for crabbing. South Jetty recommended for clamming.
13 Governor Patterson Memorial Recommended for crabbing.
14 Beachside State Recreation Site Recommended for crabbing and clamming.
15 Yachats State Recreation Area Closed to clams and mussels.
16 Cape Perpetua Closed to mussels and clams (except razor clams).
17 Neptune State Park Closed to oysters.

APPENDIX B
Oregon Coast Beaches–Southern Half

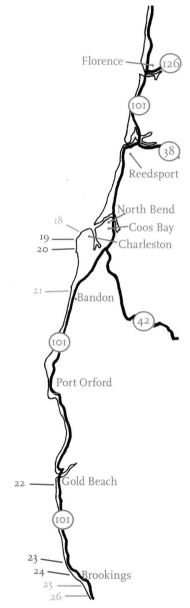

IMPORTANT NOTICE: The information on this chart is current as of the edition of this book. For the latest information on shellfish regulations and recommendations for Oregon beaches contact the Oregon Department of Fish & Wildlife: Newport (541.867.4741), Charleston (541.888.5515), or Astoria (503.325.2462).

RED TITLES: Shellfishing Restrictions imposed on this beach or area.

BLUE TITLES: Recommended as a beach or area for specific kinds of shellfishing.

18 Sunset Bay Recommended for crabbing and clamming.

19 Gregory Point Closed to shellfishing in subtidal zone (below low-water mark).

20 Cape Arago Closed to oysters.

21 Bullards Beach Recommended for crabbing.

22 Pyramid Rock (Rogue Reef) Closed to shellfishing May 1 - August 31.

23 Harris Beach Closed to shellfishing.

24 Brookings Closed to oysters.

25 McVay Rock State Recreation Site Recommended for clamming.

26 Winchuck State Recreation Site Recommended for clamming.